The Code for New Leaders

The Code for New Leaders

How to Hit the Ground Running
in Days not Weeks

Henry Rose Lee

Talenttio Books
London

First Published in Great Britain in 2015 by Talenttio Books

ISBN
978-0-9934516-0-7 (paperback)
978-0-9934516-1-4 (e-book)

Talenttio Books are available at special quantity discounts to use as premiums and sales promotions, or for use in corporate training programmes. To contact a representative please email us at books@talenttio.com.

British Library Cataloguing in Publication Data
A CIP record for this book is available from the British Library

Library of Congress Cataloging in Publication Data

Lee, Henry Rose
            The Code for New Leaders: how to hit the ground running in days not weeks

Printed and bound in Great Britain by JEM

To JB

'Leadership and learning are indispensable to each other'
John Fitzgerald Kennedy

About the Author

Henry Rose Lee started coaching on the school bus at the age of 12, when she discovered one of her friends in tears over the recent death of her mother. When everyone else was too embarrassed to talk to this girl, Henry Rose simply took her hand and sat and listened. Together, the two children grieved and giggled, plotted and planned to make their adolescent goals and dreams come true. But it was a decade or two before Henry Rose became a professional coach and got paid money for doing it.

That's Henry Rose all over; she cannot sit by and do nothing when others need some help. And that's why *The Code for New Leaders* was written.

In 2014, one of her C-suite coaching clients was struggling to succeed in a new post and she realised that all those books about leadership didn't cover those first critical days when it's 'make or break' for a new leader. Her book offers a *code of conduct* for new leaders so that they can be effective in role as quickly as possible and *not* take 90 days.

In today's high-speed, high-tech world, 90 days is far too slow. What new leaders need now is to be able to demonstrate in days that they are fit for purpose, and that they can take just enough action to reassure the people who hired or promoted them that they are proactive and strategic - and as a result win enough time and space to bed into the role and become the leader they need to be.

The Code for New Leaders is a practical guide with immediately usable tools and techniques for hitting the ground running in days not weeks.

Henry Rose Lee has worked in Corporate Leadership for 15 years. During this time, she has coached aspiring young managers to stardom. She has acted as a sounding board and confidential trusted advisor to many senior leaders. She has been the *voice of reason* providing highly sought after insights for corporate boards in their search for top talent.

She is founder of Talenttio, a company that specialises in the Tech and Financial Service sectors where the oldest and the newest can and do learn from one another. Key clients include Cisco, Criteo, Silicon Valley Bank, Legal & General, Barclays and Monitise.

In 'The Code', you'll discover how to:

- Win over the hearts and mind of key groups, teams and individuals - so that you start to build networks and connections that will support your role
- Undertake effective critical thinking - which is the foundation of all strategic analysis, planning and execution
- Maximise your available time more effectively - it may be boring but it's important
- Manage the human side of your working life - those internal sensations and emotions that can trip or hold you back
- Understand the impact you have on other people - and recognise more clearly that what you do and say has an immediate effect on others

Jam-packed with action-oriented hints and tips, and real-life case studies, *The Code for New Leaders* provides you with a route map for becoming an effective, strategic leader quickly and relatively painlessly.

Acknowledgements

Thanks to all those who helped me to write this book.

With special thanks to:

John Bessant, who used his professorial skills to step into the mind of those who might read this book.

Tim Hewitt, who gave me the idea of a chapter summary; simple yet brilliant!

Sarah Trought, who always gives me useful and constructive feedback and who always has my back.

Henry Tulip, who used his considerable intellect and attention to detail to bring some rigour to my work.

JB, who gave me the idea for the book when I realised how I should have been coaching him as a new leader; he had to find the way all by himself and he did it; I should have helped him more and I won't make that mistake again.

Phil Cox, who taught me a simple yet incredibly powerful lesson about leadership - that leaders must lead and that means learning to let go!

Ems, who always sprinkles me with kick-arse dust and no longer lets me do my own diary – I couldn't function without you Ems!

QJ, who is my counsellor, cheerleader and confidant; he has a way of making me learn, develop and raise my game. I may grumble – and I love it!

My thanks to all the readers of my previous books, blogs, papers and reports, who told me I had this book in me.

I'm grateful to you all and this book is dedicated to you all. Thanks!

Contents

Introduction

'Before you are a leader, success is all about growing yourself. When you become a leader, success is all about growing others'.

Jack Welch (Ex CEO of General Electric, consultant, speaker, author of *Winning*)

I got the call from JB late one night. He sounded upbeat – and suggested that maybe we could meet up the next time I was in London for a quick chat. He spoke to me with such an air of studied insouciance that I know he was quietly freaking out. So I managed to rearrange a couple of appointments and met him the very next day for a coffee. As a corporate trainer and coach for the past 15 years, I can sense when trouble's brewing. And having coached JB in various blue-chip organisations over a two-year period, I was keen to see how he was doing.

On the face of it, he was doing brilliantly. He had come up through the sales route and even after becoming Managing Director of the digital services arm in one group, he was unable to live down the fact that he was a cocky, outspoken, smart, salesperson and not a strategic leader. Untrue; but early mud sticks. Imagine his delight when he got a job as a new leader in a six-year old, agile and rapidly growing, cool, new-tech company. As a new UK Managing Director he believed he had left behind the salesperson label and he felt ready for massive success. So why did he need to see me? I soon found out.

JB told me that he had spent the first three months of his brand new leadership role diligently assessing the organisation and industry, checking out the management team and the sales teams and doing his homework. But now, just five months into the job, his reputation had plummeted and he was told that he was not moving fast enough and not dealing pro-actively enough with the issues of value propositions, under-performing salespeople and poor management.

As he described his troubles, he told me that he was thinking of jumping ship, having been head-hunted for a better-paid job. I got very stern with him and told him I'd be 'personally very disappointed' if he didn't tough it out. I told him he had all that he needed to be successful, he just needed to show his bosses that he was taking action.

Before our coffees got cold, JB outlined some ideas that had been swirling around in his brain: he had a lot of answers, but he hadn't realised that he needed to move quickly in order to be seen as an effective new leader. Together we debated some of his ideas and he mapped out his very next steps.

From that day, JB worked hard to make the necessary changes to his division. It was very difficult for him to overcome this early, negative reputation and it took him a further six months and a poor probationary report from his CEO and from HR to show the board that he really was an effective leader.

Is this normal? Unfortunately yes.

Is it unfair? Totally.

After just over a year in the job he has revolutionised the product and service line, has replaced the top management team and has more clearly categorised the value propositions of the sales teams. His UK division is the fastest-growing and most profitable in EMEA (Europe, the Middle East and Africa). He is now the darling of the global group. But his early activities were too slow and too tentative for him to look like he was the right man for the job. And that gave him a lot of pain.

JB is one of the major catalysts for this book. If I had written up the ideas I've been using for years to support new leaders, to help him hit the ground running in his first few days, he might well have avoided all the bad press, the crisis of faith and the unfair judgement that his first nine months in the new role brought him. All he needed was to take just enough action to reassure his bosses that he was proactive and strategic – so that they would give him the time and space he need to make longer-term changes to his business.

Of course, he's not the only reason for writing a book on leadership.

I wrote this book for two kinds of readers: the Millennial or Gen Y readers and also the Baby Boomer and Gen X readers.

Millennials/Gen Y:

First and foremost, this book is for new leaders aged between 27 and 35. In the UK, we often call these people Generation Y or 'Gen Y'. In the US and mainland Europe, the term used is Millennials – although this label is applied to people who are aged between 18 and 33. Whilst there is some disagreement over the generational term and the age bracket, the readers who will get the most out of this book are those who are the up-and-coming leaders in the Millennial/Gen Y categories. These leaders will be doing more than just managing people or projects. They will set a strategic vision and deploy a substantial budget within their organisation. They will need to lead and influence everyone around them in order to get their job done, for the benefit of their own role and that of the company.

Baby Boomers and Generation X:

This book is also for Baby Boomers, (born between 1946 and 1964), and Generation X, (born between 1965 and 1980), who are in even more senior leadership positions. These leaders are seeing much younger leaders climb the ladder far more rapidly than they did at their age. And there's a reason for that. Millennials now account for one third of the total US population, one quarter of the total UK population and one half of the population of India (see note below). Millennials are now entering the workforce in huge numbers. Not only that, Generation X is the smallest generation in most regions of the world. The birth rate boomed after the Second World War - hence the term Baby Boomers. But when these post-war children grew up, they had many fewer children than the following Generation. This means that Generation X is the smallest generation in the workplace too – currently squeezed between the Baby Boomers who don't want to retire too early and Millennials who are hungry for career progression. The result? Because Generation X is the smallest group of leaders, as they replace the finally retiring Baby Boomers, they will leave middle and senior leadership positions for the Millennials to fill.

In a study commissioned by Elance-oDesk and Millennial Branding Oct 22nd 2014, the Bureau of Labor Statistics in the USA confirmed that from 2015 Millennials are now the largest generation in the US workplace. Other countries are following suit. This means it's likely that Millennials will simply have to be promoted, since their numbers will be in greater supply than their older counterparts.

But will this newly promoted workforce be fully prepared, equipped and skilled to lead at a more senior level? They will have had far less time and experience in lower-level positions than any of the previous generations. This is a matter of great opportunity for new Millennial leaders. But it's a matter of great concern for Baby Boomers and Gen X, as they see young leaders given positions of authority when they consider them far from ready. (Source – Millennials at work survey by Pricewaterhouse Cooper UK – 2008 and 2011)

It's vital to reassure Baby Boomers and Generation X that Millennials/Generation Y can lead effectively, even if they do so at a much younger age, and with far less experience than their predecessors.

This book offers a code of conduct for new leaders to use at once so that they can be successful in role as soon as possible. And why is it a code? Well, it seems to fit well with the Wikipedia explanation of a code. 'In communications and information processing, code is a system of rules to convert information - such as a letter, word, sound, image, or gesture - into another form or representation, sometimes shortened or secret, for communication through a channel or storage in a medium.' My code for new leaders is a way to convert what I have learned and used with my clients as a route map to help them perform effectively. This code includes six key activities which new leaders can deploy – quickly and efficiently.

I have included a wide range of coaching stories and they are all assigned to two coachees whom I have called Rick and Janie. In reality, Rick and Janie don't actually exist. In the corporate world a good consultant, coach or facilitator worth their salt will have story after story of success and failure, pleasure and pain, tears and laughter. We've all got our client case studies. The problem is that for many of us in the leadership development business our clients don't want to say they've been receiving consulting, training and coaching in order to improve their leadership mind-set, attitude or behaviours. In the world of business it can be a dirty secret. I found that whilst my clients were happy to talk to me off the record few felt comfortable to go on record with their imperfections and development journey. Makes sense. It's almost like giving away the secret recipe for Coca Cola. It's part of your winning formula.

So I have invented Rick and Janie who are an amalgam of the all the new leaders I have ever worked with and with whom I still work. I present their trials and tribulations in order to show what new leaders do as they navigate the choppy waters of work whilst sailing their ship towards the agreed destination. Like all my clients, Rick and Janie are doing their best to avoid a ship-wreck on the corporate rocks.

Rick represents the glamorous, sexy teenager of the technology world with its youthful vigour and boundless energy and enthusiasm. Janie represents the centuries-old financial services sector, with its conventions and regulations. Both are in their early 30s and both have gained promotion rapidly.

And before you decide this book is not for you, because you don't work in the digital or the financial services market place, think again. The financial services organisations portrayed by Janie's stories actually represent all the mature, well-established organisations who have been around for generations – such as retailing, production, manufacturing and pharmaceuticals. The technology and digital sector as depicted by Rick's stories actually relate to any organisation that has only been around for only a few years – a toddler in business years if you like.

The combined stories of Rick and Janie help me to share with you the true-life stories of the people I have actually worked with; the new leaders who are shaping the world of business and whose success and achievements will develop, probably literally, the economy and the culture of the world in years to come. What they do is important, real-world and life-changing.

If you are a new leader, like Rick and Janie, you'll see that they're walking the world in shoes like yours and looking at business with the same eyes as you. They are also thinking about business as usual and strategies for the future with a brain like yours. They are Millennials - aged between 27 and 35, like you. They are you.

In working with the Ricks and the Janies of the technology and financial services sectors I have developed an overarching methodology for propelling these new leaders into early success. Using 'The Code' outlined in this book, I help them to get immediate wins, deliver clear communications and take deliberate actions, which ensure they hit the ground running quickly as new leaders.

My code includes six activities for new leaders which are all about taking rapid, jam-packed action. Clearly, this pace is very intense and 'The Code' is specifically designed to work quickly and to get the leader into a position rapidly where they have a plan, a list of actions to undertake and a sense of motivation and momentum that drives them forward effectively, in record time.

The Code for New Leaders includes three positioning chapters – for those analytical readers who want lots of context and background.

Chapter 1 positions the importance and value of leadership.

Chapter 2 answer the question 'Why do we need new leaders in business?'

Chapter 3 introduces you to the old lady and the teenager – who represent all forms of business – from the highly mature, been-around-for-ever organisations – through to the babies of the business world – from start-ups to early IPO (initial public offering).

Chapter 4 explains how vital the first few days of a new leader's tenure can be – do you want to step up and look like a leader at once? Do you want to reassure the people who employed or promoted you? Do you want them to look good and feel good about having given you the job? If you don't think about your first few days, you may well cock up – just like JB – and we all know how painful that can be.

Chapter 5 describes the three-pronged DNA that sits behind 'The Code'; your authenticity, attitude and actions. Get these right and you will look like, walk like and talk like the leader you want to be.

From Chapter 6 to Chapter 11, the six activities of 'The Code' for new leaders is laid out in full.

Chapter 6 brings you Activity 1: winning over groups and teams. It explains how you can win over key teams via a combination of management by walking about (MBWA) and team surgeries (team meetings which are open-door, fact-finding sessions, designed to win over as many people as possible).

Chapter 7 outlines Activity 2: winning over key individuals. It demonstrates how you can win over the most important individuals in your organisation. The good news is that you don't have to win over every single client, team member, line manager or stakeholder. You just have to win over the ones with the most power and influence.

Chapter 8 covers Activity 3: critical thinking. It positions the importance of strategic thinking, explaining what it is, and how to do it effectively.

Chapter 9 deals with Activity 4: time management. No one ever thinks this is important. And it is. It will be your least favourite chapter and one of the most important. Force yourself to read it. Then do what it suggests. It will help. It really will.

Chapter 10 explains Activity 5: understanding your impact on others. It raises your awareness about the consequences of everything you say and do; it's all going to influence the words and actions of others. When dealing with the key people in your workplace, you need to think carefully about their needs and their issues. Ignore these at your peril.

Chapter 11 brings you Activity 6: managing how you think and feel at work. It deals with those sensations and emotions that are inside all human beings that can trip us up and hold us back. Deal with these and you will automatically become a better leader.

Chapter 12 is the final chapter where I'm asking you to try out at least some of the tools and techniques in this book. Choose the elements that work for you and do something quickly and decisively. As long as it's just enough to make a small, yet effective difference, and it's just enough to get the attention of the key players, you'll hit the ground running in days not weeks.

And what about all the other books on leadership? Well, I have great respect for other books for new leaders. Michael D. Watkins' book *The First 90 Days* is a must-read for any new leader. It has some first-rate advice, hints and tips for managing the first few months; it is practical and results-oriented. As Watkins says about leaders who are promoted or employed into a new leadership role, 'Transitions are critical times when small differences in your actions can have disproportionate impacts on results. Leaders, regardless of their level, are most vulnerable in their first few months in a new position because they lack detailed knowledge of the challenges they will face and what it will take to succeed in meeting them; they also have not yet developed a network of relationships to sustain them. Failure to create momentum during the first few months virtually guarantees an uphill battle for the rest of your tenure in the job'.

Watkins' book is fantastic for new leaders, whether they are new to their senior role or they are already a leader and joining a new organisation or a new industry. It provides a practical, immediately usable blueprint for new leaders to ensure they are effective.

But there's a problem with it; it takes too long to deliver a confident, pro-active, new leader who can hit the ground running and take action now.

The Code for New Leaders is the pre-requisite to this 'do-it-in-90 days' book. 'The Code' helps new leaders to walk like, talk like, look like and act like someone who is right for the job, someone who is worth following. It buys new leaders the time to follow the principles of the other wonderful leadership books in the market place. It gives them a chance to have the space to learn more about their role, whilst starting immediately to make a difference as a newbie. 'The Code' ensures the new leader will deal with current Business as Usual (BAU) and move quickly into setting and dealing with strategic objectives during the initial stages of their tenure, so that they can become the effective, successful leaders that they, and the companies that employ them, want them to be.

Chapter 1

Leadership can save your life

On 18th December 2008, five Eurostar services broke down inside the Channel Tunnel during snowy weather, trapping around 2,400 people. The trains fell prey to a particular weather problem; very cold weather outside the fifty-four kilometre tunnel running between Folkestone and Calais and high temperatures inside the tunnel, causing the electrics to malfunction. No trains ran until 22nd December and services remained disrupted up to Christmas. It was about that time that I was asked by Eurotunnel, who own and operate the Channel Tunnel, to look into how best to manage customer service with passengers on the Eurotunnel trains under crisis and emergency situations. Just how do you deal with over 1000 people and their cars inside a train that has lost power if you have to evacuate them all in an orderly and safe fashion? In the dark!

To be clear, Eurotunnel and Eurostar have always had fantastic security and safety measures in place and are continually investing in training and equipment designed to ensure the continued protection and security of their customers. Their safety and recovery record is impressive.

However, back in 2008 the issue was one of dealing with the people side of the issue; what to say, how to say it and what to do in order to avoid mass panic, anger, fear or inadvisable behaviour. In preparation for the training programme that I developed and ran for Eurotunnel I read two books; *Survival Psychology* by Dr John Leach and *The Survivors Club* by Ben Sherwood. First published in 1994 and 2009 respectively, these fascinating, but frankly terrifying, books changed some of my views on leadership completely.

Both books deal with disasters such as 9/11 in 2001, Hurricane Katrina in 2005 and the Kings Cross fire in 1987 and there is much that we can learn about how people lead and can be led during times of emergency, trauma and crisis.

Two key lessons:

> 1.   People tend to try to think and act normally, the brain's normalcy bias, even when a situation is abnormal or when they don't understand what is happening, the incredulity bias. (The normalcy bias was a term first coined by Richard Thaler in 1980 – an economist and Professor of Behavioral Science and Economics. Both the normalcy bias and the incredulity bias was first written about by Kahnemann, Thaler et al in their studies on behavioural finance.) Most people want to be led; either out of danger, or into a more comfortable and 'normal' situation.

2.   Neuroscientific research has shown that the brain stores experiences and reactions in the long-term memory. And since we don't meet difficult and unexpected events or even crises or emergencies every day, most people tend to find that when the tough, new situation or the emergency occurs, they don't recognise it and can't explain it and they don't know what to do. Therefore, the brain gives them no response and no action command. These people may simply freeze or carry on with what they are doing. When people freeze, this is often called brain-lock.

Brain-lock was a term first used by Dr John Leach in his book *Survival Psychology* to describe a phenomenon in sky-diving where the brain can seize up under moments of stress. It is easy to understand how, during a sky-dive, especially the person's first ever jump, when the heart is pounding, blood pressure is higher and stress hormones are pumping, that the human brain can literally seize up or freeze for a few seconds. Under such circumstances some sky-divers can literally forget where they are and what they are doing. They might even forget to pull their rip cord. Surprisingly, brain-lock is normal and can happen to anyone under stress, even under routine circumstances at work or at home. Have you ever made a key-note presentation to a huge audience and forgotten what to say next? That's momentary brain-lock. Usually the brain recovers after a few seconds.

But if the information is impossible for the person to understand and they cannot move past brain-lock they will attempt to normalise the situation, which means carrying on as normal, as if nothing different has happened.

CCTV footage from the 1987 Kings Cross underground station fire in London showed commuters buying tickets and travelling down escalators despite smoke pouring out of the station. As one observer put it, the commuters 'wanted a normal journey so they simply tuned out anything that contradicted that notion, such as the fire'. When the planes hit the Twin Towers in 2001, some workers refused to leave their work-posts and calmly carried on sending emails and completing reports. It seem that, at least for some of them, their brains could not cope with something they had never met before, so they just continued to do what they usually did. And they died.

When Hurricane Katrina hit New Orleans in 2005 of the people who died the majority were over sixty. Having experienced and survived hurricanes before, these older citizens had always remained in their houses, battened down the hatches and waited for the storm to pass. They stayed put because they could not comprehend doing anything else. They could not believe that the levees (embankments) would fail or that this hurricane was more dangerous than the others. They stayed at home believing they could sit out the hurricane. And some of them died.

People don't just go into brain-lock during times of crisis, disaster or even emergency attacks. Most of us want to 'carry on as normal' rather than having to deal with any upsetting or frightening news. For example, when the global recession took hold in 2008 thousands of people lost their jobs, yet despite warning signs in their companies many people didn't search for new jobs or prepare for unemployment until they actually got fired or were made redundant. They didn't plan for the future until it arrived. And that's when it's too late.

In order to understand why it's important that people are led it's useful to look at Dr John Leach's '10 80 10 rule'. Dr John Leach is a leading expert on survival psychology. His theory is based on years of research of various emergencies and incidents and after serving as a reserve officer in the Royal Air Force, including a tour in Iraq in 2003. He specialises in teaching the military how to survive in every kind of environment. His research has led him to develop the theory of 10 80 10. It's a rough yet useful rule of thumb. It's based on 10% of people who act as leaders and take action, 75% to 80% of people who require leadership and look for someone else to tell them what to do or where to go, and the 5% to 10% of people who can potentially do something wrong, silly or risky under unexpected or uncertain circumstances.

The 10% who take action: In emergencies around 10% of people will handle a crisis in a relatively calm and rational state of mind. Under pressure these people pull themselves together quickly. They assess situations clearly. Their decision-making is sharp and focused. They are able to develop priorities, make plans and take appropriate action. These people are not heroes or heroines. They are simply able to recover from brain-lock more rapidly than others. They do this by having a more fluid approach to what is considered normal. That means they can respond positively to any new circumstances quickly and start to process and make decisions about what, in effect, has become the new normal. This behaviour also uses the 'normalcy bias' but it does it in a more adaptable and flexible way.

The 80% who freeze: Up to 80% of people in emergencies end up becoming stunned and confused. Their mental reasoning is significantly impaired and they find thinking very difficult. They behave in a reflexive, almost automatic or mechanical manner. They experience 'tunnel vision' and barely see or hear anything around them. They may even feel lethargic, numb or sick. They freeze and take no action because their brain is undergoing the 'incredulity response'. If you ever see someone freeze up in this way you can help by asking them to recite the alphabet or to tell you what they had for breakfast or dinner last night. If you can, get them to do a simple task such as making a cup of tea of coffee. All these activities encourage the brain to move past brain-lock and to find some acceptable and safe normalcy, which will then allow them to start functioning properly again).

The 10% who do the wrong thing: According to Dr Leach, the remaining 10% appear to do the wrong thing. They may experience panic, even hysteria and they may burst into tears and start screaming or running away. Others might be rooted to the spot, unable to move or speak. Worse still, others may behave counter-intuitively; for example they might run towards the danger instead of away from it. They can make difficult situations worse by their unexpected behaviour.

What this all means:

Most human beings need leadership, particularly in times of crisis or stress. Since only 10% of people at any time will act like leaders in a given situation, this means that most people will require someone to act as a leader; someone who will step up, speak out and provide some direction and normalcy.

Here are some amazing examples of leadership:

The 2001 attack on the Twin Towers in New York (9/11)

No one ever asks how many people survived from the two planes hitting the twin towers in New York on September 11th 2001. Did you know that during any 24-hour period up to 100,000 people were coming and going inside the two towers? On that dreadful day it is estimated that between 15,000 and 19,000 people escaped unharmed.

How did this happen? Leadership. Many of those people who survived had been taught by leaders what to do and how to do it in the event of an emergency; including how to escape and how to follow emergency safety procedures. Some of those who escaped under exceptional and amazing circumstances were led to safety.

One particularly poignant story is surely that of British-born Cyril Richard 'Rick' Rescorla, (May 27 1939 – September 11 2001). A retired USA army officer, Rescorla was the Director of Security for the financial services firm Morgan Stanley at the World Trade Center. With incredible prescience Rescorla had anticipated both attacks on the towers and had implemented regular evacuation procedures and rehearsals. When the first plane hit the North Tower on 11th September Rescorla ignored the Port Authority announcement which told workers to stay at their desks. He systematically ordered Morgan Stanley employees to evacuate, including the 1,000 employees in building WTC 5 and also 250 people visiting nearby offices for a stockbroker training class. After successfully evacuating most of Morgan Stanley's 2,687 employees he went back into the building to continue helping others just before the South Tower collapsed. His body was never recovered.

2005 Hurricane Katrina

Hurricane Katrina is noted for being one of the costliest natural disasters in the USA's history, and one of the deadliest Atlantic hurricanes ever. 1,836 people died, most of them over 60 years of age, during the hurricane and the subsequent floods. Most of the deaths occurred in New Orleans, Louisiana, which flooded after the flood prevention system, levees, failed. The people over 60 years old who were saved were literally carried and dragged onto the boats by 'leaders' who knew these people needed to be moved and they took the decision to move them, whether or not they had permission.

Whilst it is unlikely that you will be called upon to save lives or undertake acts of outstanding bravery in your lifetime, these stories demonstrate that without leadership most people will face situations that they don't know how to deal with. The awful news might not be a hurricane or a terrorist attack but it might be bad enough to produce the same crisis behaviour in the brain, whether that is brain-lock, the incredulity bias or the desperate search for normalcy. After the worst global recession in living memory the recovery has been painfully slow and many people are earning 20% less than they were before the recession began, whilst working twice as hard. It's still bad out there in places. It's not suddenly going to get better. Some people still feel lost and listless, shafted and scared, rudderless and leaderless.

Do bear in mind that I'm not suggesting that you suddenly become an autocratic, aggressive, I'm-in-front-follow-me sort of leader. That may work in times of emergency. What I am pointing out is that human beings often need a direction to go. They often need something which gives them momentum, stimulus and context. They need engagement and motivation. Leadership can do all of that. And if you want to be the leader those are the actions and behaviours that the people following you will be looking for.

What the horror and sadness of crisis have taught us all is that leadership makes a difference. It really does. And it can save your life.

Takeaways

1. Under stress, crisis, emergency or upsetting conditions, everything from a life-threatening storm to fear of job losses, many people can stop thinking normally and need someone else to take charge.

2. History has shown us that leadership is vital for humans. Most of us want to be led and want to have lives that are normal (normalcy bias) and understandable (avoiding the incredulity bias).

3. When leaders step up they can positively impact the people around them and the situations in which they find themselves. Leadership makes a difference. Leadership can save a life.

Chapter 2

Why do we need new leaders in business?

And why do they have to hit the ground running so quickly?

Why all the fuss about new leaders? The most recent data around UK leadership has reached the following conclusions:

1. The perceptions and the research about organisational leadership are equally damning. They state that organisational leadership in the UK is not currently good enough and is nowhere near ready for the continuous global commercial and economic changes being faced by businesses today. This judgement is not restricted to the UK; equally negative feedback about leadership is also coming out of other countries.

2. Global trust in business is at an all-time low, and it's likely to be the role of the new, up-and-coming leaders to rebuild that trust from the top down and from the inside out.

3.   Generation Y is growing up all over the world; and they're taking over new leadership roles. As true digital natives, having grown up with technology, against an economic background of boom (1980s and 1990s), to bust (2007 onwards) their experiences and education are likely to mean they lead in a very different way.

4.   Global   technology,   transport, communications and media have created a world that is flat – metaphorically. Information, intelligence and trending can now move so fast that change is a constant norm rather than an unwanted exception. Not only is today's news tomorrow's fish and chip paper, it often has an almost built-in obsolescence as we chase the new, the novel, the now. Leadership must change too. (Source: *The World is Flat – a brief history of the twenty-first century* by Thomas L. Friedman. Friedman believes the world is flat because the competition between first world markets and emerging markets is becoming level. Competition, supply chains, distribution and communication can be local and global and often span continents. That makes many business people feel we can reach out and touch anywhere in the world so it might as well be flat).

Research on UK Leadership from the Chartered Management Institute

In early 2014, the Commission on the Future of Management and Leadership was sponsored by the Chartered Management Institute to look into leadership. In July that year it published its report 'Management 2020 – Leadership to unlock long-term growth[1]'. From the sixty-page report I have found five compelling reasons for having improved new leadership.

The UK lags behind many competitors on key economic indicators

Productivity is 21% lower than that of the rest of the G7 countries.[2] The UK is also measured at lower levels of achievement than many other European nations. In addition, the report states that time wasted by poor management could be costing the UK economy as much as £19bn a year.[3]

Younger generations will drive new ways of working

'Generation Y' and 'Millennials' will make up 75% of the workforce by 2025. Their expectations about the employment relationship and ways of working demand new approaches. There are also major employability challenges for young people in the UK. Generation Y[4] in the UK are positioned as people born in the 1980s and 1990s and Millennials are people born from 2000 onwards.[5]

---

1   http://bit.ly/1MG4YXK

2   Statistical Bulletin: International Comparisons of Productivity – Final Estimates, 2012, ONS, 20 February 2014

3   Leadership and management in the UK – The key to sustainable growth, Department for Business, Innovation & Skills, July 2012

4   http://bit.ly/1MG5i9d

5   http://bit.ly/1HdWPIu

Managers will need to be adequately trained

Government data shows that the UK labour market will need one million new managers by 2020 yet 71% of the leaders surveyed by the Chartered Management Institute confess they could do better at training first-time managers, or don't train them at all. This could leave 150,000 employees a year taking on management roles without adequate preparation.

Technology demands better people skills

New technology doesn't only demand new technical skills, increased connectivity between people puts a premium on the need for the leaders to have excellent personal, communication, network-building and collaboration skills. Leaders need to articulate their own vision and align it to the vision of their company, whilst providing a context into the marketplace for customers, stakeholders, shareholders and colleagues. There has never been such a need for communication and teamwork, both of which often get blurred, distorted or deleted behind technology. From email to sales process and social media to IT storage, the human element is what makes the difference. The human element is the leader.

Long-term sustainability is fundamental

The global economic crash exposed the danger posed by short-termism in management thinking and incentives. Those who cut costs and overheads still seem to earn more respect than those who take the riskier, more innovative paths that lead to growth in revenue, profits and jobs. Leaders need to define their organisation's long-term purpose and resist pressure for short-term results.

The damning perceptions about leadership

Like many children of the 1970s and 1980s as world travel opened up we started taking holidays and working in other countries. Having experienced many cultures and languages I have learned that it's not just UK leaders who are starting to struggle with the leadership that's required for a new world.

The damning 'home truths' about poor UK leadership that I've heard were summed up for me by Gerry Lemberg, a Russian-American Israeli with whom I worked a few years ago. Gerry was thirteen when he met a very old and still fascinating Albert Einstein. This historic meeting inspired Gerry to study quantum mechanics. He worked through a number of successful careers including management and leadership posts in the corporate world and a university professorship, before getting involved in start-ups. He came relatively late in life to the world of corporate people development and his decades of business and educational experience culminated in him living and working in the UK. Gerry often talked to me about the inability of the UK to lead projects and people successfully; he believed it was due to what he cuttingly called 'The Four Horsemen of the Apocalypse and his Dog'. Unfortunately, whilst Gerry has rather unfairly stereotyped UK leadership in a negative and derogatory fashion, he was not alone in his thoughts. Having first met him at a corporate university working party conference, he became a regular to my corporate university working party meetings. He never changed his thoughts on the UK business culture, but – right up until his death in 2006, he remained an active supporter of UK start-ups and was closely linked to the London Business School of entrepreneurship activities. Here is how he used to sum up the British leadership style.

> **The Four Horsemen of the Apocalypse**
>
> The four horseman of the apocalypse are described in the Bible as the four beings on horses that symbolize conquest, war, famine and death and who will ride out as the world comes to an end and judgement day is reached. According to the last book of the New Testament these horsemen will cause the death of most of the population since most will be judged to be wanting and not worthy of the kingdom of God. So that's not saying anything kind about UK leadership! As for the dog...

According to Gerry, these five characteristics have an impact on any initiative, including the worthy effort of leading people. The British:

1. Live in the past.
2. Are risk-averse.
3. View failure as terminal.
4. Value form over substance.
5. Have a blame culture.

1 The British live in the past

Gerry asserted that when compared with North America and Asia Pacific the UK tends to keep too many old and anachronistic systems and processes. These might be hundreds of years old and are firmly embedded in the UK psyche; yet they serve no real purpose in the 21st century. One example Gerry gave me was around two British working practices which are extinct in the USA. The first is scaffolding and the other is white-line painting. In the UK these two archaic systems still exist and are both highly labour-intensive, even with the introduction of new machinery. In the US these practices have both been replaced by technology and virtually no staff. When comparing the UK to the US, Gerry believes that Americans celebrate their past with pride but will also look clearly to the future. The US culture is built on people who left 'the old world' for 'the new world' and who are more open-minded, flexible and entrepreneurial.

2 The British are risk-averse

British corporations and employees have often been viewed as being highly risk-averse. Even at school people are encouraged to 'take part' and to enjoy taking part rather than competing aggressively and beating others to win. The 2012 Olympics proved that the UK loves to win, but Gerry's view was that most people, particularly in the business world, play reactively in order not to lose, rather than play proactively in order to win. In the US psyche winning is valued and prized. Gerry often quoted Vince Lombardi, a celebrated American football coach, who said: 'Winning isn't everything, it's the only thing.''

3 The British view failure as terminal

The Japanese concept of 'Kaizen' relates to the practice of continuous improvement and change for the best. This first saw light after the Second World War when American business practices, including quality management and time and motion analysis, were copied and then bettered by Japanese companies. Kaizen has led to the reduction of waste and to the simplification and streamlining of systems and procedures, including business management and leadership. The Japanese also have a term - Kintsugi - which I will loosely translate as 'failing forward' or celebrating the learning that can be taken from mistakes. (Kintsugi is the Japanese art of repairing broken pottery with lacquer dusted or mixed with powdered gold, silver, or platinum – so even when something gets broken, it can be mended with something beautiful; what a great definition for learning from your cock-ups!)

According to Gerry, in other cultures successful people are hailed as much for the fact that they have failed as for having succeeded. After the North American dot-com bubble burst many new tech entrepreneurs failed in their ventures, but they were re-employed by other US corporations almost immediately because it was believed that they would have useful lessons to share with others. Back in the UK, the recent debacle of the banking system proves that not only are some corporates viewed as 'too big to fail', but also those workers who have been fired or made redundant are often viewed with more negativity than those who have chosen to change jobs whilst still in full-time employment. In the UK, failure is bad; failure is viewed as the end of things, rather than part of the process.

4 The British value form over substance

Many people think that the UK still uses outmoded, old-fashioned business practices because 'it's always been like that'. British-run companies, employees and even entrepreneurs are viewed as having a love of tradition which stops them accepting something new that will bring benefits. We can talk all we like about new technologies and new ways of doing things but the productivity ladder makes depressing reading. Labour productivity, which is the amount of economic output each worker generates per hour, fell sharply in the UK during the global recession and has remained weak to this day, particularly in comparison with the rest of Europe. Economists believe that this is largely due to employers hanging on to workers when output fell and then hiring more people, even part-time workers, when the economy was stagnant.

There are several factors to watch. As well as the evolution of economic output and employment, economists will be looking for a recovery in business investment which should lead to productivity gains.

The British have a blame culture

Gerry's particular bug-bear was around blame. Gerry saw the UK as having a persistent blame-culture. When something goes wrong many employers and employees look for something or someone to blame. There is a 'gotcha' culture in the UK and many instances where someone has to be the 'scapegoat'. Take a look at our British newspapers and tell me we don't like to blame others! Worse still, with over fifteen years of experience working in the financial services I have found that most investment and wealth management institutions in the UK are living with the fear every day that they will be blamed if revenues drop, or clients jump ship. This culture of fear creates a dangerous cocktail of analysis-paralysis and the fears of whistle-blowing and recrimination. People keep silent. People under-play their potential.

It doesn't really matter whether you agree with Gerry. When he first put forward his four horsemen and their dog to a group of blue chip companies in London the room was divided and raucous. In addition, when I sent this book to various beta readers in the US, Ireland, Sweden and Germany, I found that most of Gerry's horsemen (and his dog) were insults that were hurled at many countries across the globe. What matters is that anyone might have negative thoughts about leadership in any country and about how leaders run the world of business and how they support or grow the economic output of their countries. In my opinion the only thing that can kill off this negative view of the UK or of any other country is the leadership that companies develop in the guts of their organisations.

A report from Right Management undertaken in 2013 found that low employee engagement and productivity were key concerns for 31% of UK executives compared to only 21% of HR professionals globally. The research surveyed 2,600 senior HR executives across 14 countries and found the UK's concerns about staff engagement and productivity were in sharp contrast to other nations surveyed. Mark Hodgson, talent management practice leader, Right Management, comments: "There's a stark contrast between levels of optimism and engagement in the UK and Europe, compared to the Americas and Asia-Pac. It seems many organisations in the UK are still stuck in recession mode but the fact is, the economy is in recovery. Businesses need to start talking about growth and start investing in and inspiring their workforce; putting talent initiatives on hold simply isn't an option."

Trust in Business Has Declined

Every year the world's largest PR Company, Edelman, publishes its global Trust Barometer. In its report of 2014 I found disappointing statistics about CEOs.

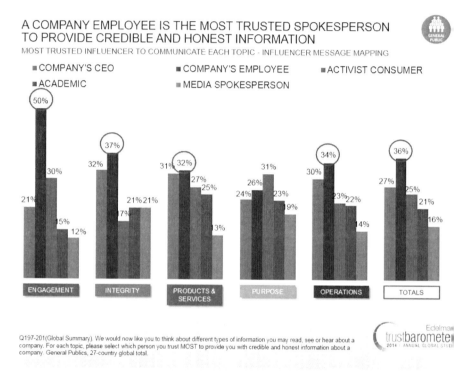

A COMPANY EMPLOYEE IS THE MOST TRUSTED SPOKESPERSON TO PROVIDE CREDIBLE AND HONEST INFORMATION

MOST TRUSTED INFLUENCER TO COMMUNICATE EACH TOPIC - INFLUENCER MESSAGE MAPPING

- COMPANY'S CEO
- COMPANY'S EMPLOYEE
- ACTIVIST CONSUMER
- ACADEMIC
- MEDIA SPOKESPERSON

Q197-201(Global Summary). We would now like you to think about different types of information you may read, see or hear about a company. For each topic, please select which person you trust MOST to provide you with credible and honest information about a company. General Publics, 27-country global total.

trustbarometer

Source: Edelman. Used with permission.

The Trust Barometer has found that a company employee is the most trusted spokesperson to provide credible and honest information to clients and customers. In their survey Edelman found that the CEO scores lower than employees but overall somewhat higher than an activist consumer, an academic or a media spokesperson.

Edelman's response to these findings is to suggest that the CEO has a role to play in becoming the Chief Engagement Officer, using their leadership position to build engagement, rapport, connection, trust and belief between their companies and their clients, customers and other stakeholders.

Don't wait until you become a CEO. Start now. Start to engage and connect and rebuild. After all, leadership is always about people first, not things.

The *Y* factor

In my life-time we've gone from having the telephone, to the telex, through to fax and pagers, to the first computers, emails, mobile texts and instant messaging and then on to social media, which now occurs largely on tablets and smartphones. The way we communicate has changed radically. Such communication developments reflect the changes that have gone on in the world around us and the world is changing again.

The economy is changing

How organisations make profits is changing. As corporations get bigger many of them have to get to near zero profits. Competition is rife. The freemium world has turned key industries such as music, publishing and even learning upside-down with many people refusing to pay for content and most expecting a great deal of content for free. This might mean that we either have huge companies with monopolies that can set pricing and therefore profits as they wish, or lots of smaller companies that struggle to make the profits of the past. The corporation market is shrinking. (Freemium is portmanteau word for a business model whereby a product or service (which is often online), is provided to a consumer without charge (free), and money is charged for additional goods, or extra functionality or increased access (premium).

Check the facts. The Global Policy Forum published a report in July 2014 which compared the revenues of the highest revenue-generating corporations with GDP. In 2010, Wal-Mart's revenues were equal to Norway's GDP. Both Exxon Mobil and Chevron had higher revenues than the entire GDP of Romania. Even after the financial crisis of 2007, American banks such as Bank of America, JP Morgan Chase, Citigroup, and Wells Fargo remain in the top 20 of the world's largest corporations, each with revenues higher than Iraq's GDP. Costco's revenue was greater than the total GDP of Luxembourg.

Technology is changing

For every new piece of technology 100s and sometimes 1,000s of jobs will be lost forever. This means that there is a real danger that some young, educated people won't get jobs and certainly won't get promotion. The job market is shrinking and becoming more competitive.

Old leadership won't cope with these changes. Old leadership learned to lead in a boom and bust, capitalist society. Old leadership grew up in a corporation that says:

- if you work hard you achieve;
- if you work in an organisation long enough you'll move up the ladder of promotion;
- if you create a good product and have economies of scale in your production line you will be successful and profitable.

No one is really sure what the future commercial world will look like. Will we all be working from home with virtual desks and video-conferencing? Will we develop lots of smaller, collaborative business communities where barter and exchange become the norm and our products and services are valued in a different way?

Whatever happens, things will change. If you're a new leader you will have grown up in the world of technology, social media and political atheism. If you are in your mid to late 20s or your early 30s as a new leader you are part of the Generation Y group. You are used to change. You are used to the new, the novel and the now. It's your norm.

The Management 2020 report from the CMI has these statistics:

- By 2025 Generation Y will comprise 75% of the global workforce.

- Generation Y looks for ethical employers, opportunities for progression, a good work-life balance and interesting work.

- More than half (57%) of UK members of Generation Y intend to leave their jobs within one to two years of joining.

- Generation Y is very comfortable with technology and social networks. It is also creative and open-minded, multi-culturally aware, confident, able to collaborate and ethical.

- But it can display a strong sense of entitlement, an inability to communicate face-to-face, a lack of decision-making skills, a poor sense of awareness, a low work ethic and a tendency towards over-confidence.

- Generation Y lacks a global mind-set. Just one UK student studies abroad for every fifteen international students who come to the UK for study.

- More than three-quarters (77%) of Generation Y view formal management qualifications to be the most effective method of learning and development.

- Entrepreneurialism is very attractive to Generation Y. More than a quarter (27%) of sixteen to thirty year olds in the UK claimed that they were increasingly thinking of setting up a business, according to 2012 research by The Prince's Trust.

If you're a new, young leader you won't function like the older leaders. Your circumstances, education and experiences make you think in a very different way.

Does this look or sound like you? Is the concept of leadership something you never considered until you realised you were about to become one?

But now you are a leader (or about to become one) are you ready? Is the world ready for you? How will you hit the ground running in days rather than weeks?

Leadership today is immediate, now, right now. It's not about sitting and waiting. Technological advances in transportation, distribution, communication, media, processing and work-load mean that everything has speeded up. New leaders have the energy and the rapid reflexes to deal with this increased pace of working. But they don't always have the tools.

New leaders have to use their natural turn of speed and their youthful vigour to lead in a new way. You are required to do the right things at the right time; and as soon as possible please. Right now. At once. Stand up. Your time has come.

Takeaways

1. Perceptions about leadership in the UK, and probably globally, are not particularly complimentary. In fact, they can be quite damning, with talk of companies living in the past, being risk-averse, valuing form over substance, seeing failure as terminal and having a blame culture.

2. With trust in business at an all-time low after the global recession the new, up-and-coming leaders will need to rebuild trust and develop new ways of leading to avoid copying the mistakes of the recent past. New leaders are likely to be Generation Y, (or Millennials). These are people born in the 80s and 90s. The first truly digitally native generation is now entering the workforce in droves and is likely to be aged between eighteen and thirty-four. As these people become leaders their upbringing, education and tech-savvy nature will mean they act, speak and lead in a new and different way. They like to multi-task, think and work rapidly and they enjoy variety and flexibility in their work environment. This is good news since global transport, media and communications have created in many corporates a sense that the world is flat.

Chapter 3

The old lady and the teenager

Imagine you're on a bus and you notice an elderly lady sitting opposite a teenager. You've got time on your hands, the bus is stuck in traffic. So you watch these two people and start to judge them. You are human after all and people-watching is great fun, especially when you're waiting to do something else, like getting off at the next stop.

So you stare and begin your mental inventory and your internal dialogue, starting with the old lady.

She looks good. She was obviously beautiful when she was young and she still makes the best of herself. She is expensively turned out and well-dressed. Great shoes. Fantastic handbag. But she is old. Really, really old. Her hands are gnarled and even the best make-up cannot hide those wrinkles and the wispy, thinning hair. By her clothes, mannerisms and behaviour she seems really set in her ways and regularly throws out looks of scorn and superiority at everyone else on the bus. Don't they now how to sit and wait? Don't they know how to behave? Every now and again, the old lady speaks. She has a good, clear voice and booms out her messages. No shy and retiring flower here. She speaks well. She has views and beliefs and is happy to share them with anyone who will listen. She'll even correct your grammar.

Now you look at the teenager, slouching nonchalantly in his seat. On his feet are a pair of Converse trainers which might have cost him a lot of money but, frankly the rest of his clothes are a hotchpotch, with a distinct charity-shop feel. He's wearing surfer shorts, in winter and as a sop to the cold he's also wearing a number of T-shirts and a hoodie. Pointless telling him he'd be warmer with trousers and a coat and scarf, he obviously dresses for his beliefs, rather than the weather. He's listening to the latest music on the most up-to-date sound equipment and he's busily avoiding contact with anyone else on the bus. They simply don't get him, so what's the point in talking to them? But if you engage him in conversation he has some surprisingly interesting things to say, that's if you can translate what he is saying into a language that the rest of the bus can understand. Now imagine that the bus is the world of business, industry and commerce. The old lady represents the financial services sector.

And the youngster on the bus is the young prince of technology, the new breed and impatient for change and something new. This kid is already a legend in his own lunch-time and prince of all he surveys. They are both on the bus as they connect with each other over money. It's not exactly the easiest of relationships. The old lady finds it hard to prove to herself that there is real value in intellectual property and totally new technologies; the young teenager gets easily frustrated and bad-tempered about all the bureaucracy and red tape that stall his brilliant ideas.

The Definition of Financial Services

Financial services are the economic services provided by the finance industry, which encompasses a broad range of organisations that manage money. These include credit unions, banks, building societies, credit card companies, insurance companies, accountancy companies, consumer finance companies, stock brokerages, investment funds etc.

Finance is big business. It is estimated that the US finance industry comprised only 10% of total non-farm business profits in 1947 but even after the crash by 2010 it represented 50%. As for the UK, even after the recession it remains a power-house in the global financial services industry. By 2014 both New York and London claimed to be the world's largest financial centre. Whoever wins that prize today, it is clear that London continues to have a key role on the global financial stage. (Source: Financial Times Article 1st October 2014 'New York and London vie for crown of world's top financial centre' by Michael Pooler)

The Definition of the Technology and Digital Technology Sectors

The technology sector provides specialised technology-oriented solutions by combining the processes and functions of software, hardware, networks, telecommunications and electronics. In the IT industry, technology services are delivered according to business or enterprise requirements. Services range from basic Internet connectivity to enterprise application (EA) software. Technology service providers include Internet service providers (ISP), application service providers (ASP), cloud providers and developers. Digital and technology services also include elements such as:

Scientific and engineering knowledge that deals with the creation and practical use of digital or computerised devices, methods and systems.

Digital devices, processes, methodologies and systems which were created by using such knowledge, such as the Internet.

Hardware, software development, integration and maintenance.

Networking integration, management and maintenance.

Information security such as data protection, fraud prevention and detection etc.

Technology companies are the newest and youngest kids on the block, teenagers. Until they get big, like a Cisco or an Experian, they just might need the old lady's money. Sometimes their passion, energy and youthful exuberance will win over the ageing *grande dame*. The young prince will be looking around his princedom for crowd-funding, venture capitalists, angels and private investors. However, sooner or later the big bucks of the key, global financial players tend to get connected with the up-and-coming technologies, so there is likely to be some connection between the old lady and the good-looking kid.

The teenager is young, beautiful and sees himself as virtually bomb-proof – strong enough to withstand any pressure and challenge. He is often arrogant and a bit sulky; he wants to be loved for who he is and what he does, although he isn't always able to get people to pay attention or to see beneath the zany and somewhat unconventional exterior. As for the old lady she still feels a bit like a queen, one who has ruled for a long time. She has seen it all; feast, famine, war and pestilence, and still she survives. With her money and her experience, often knowing how best to run the game; when to hold, when to bet and when to play. In her quest for continued survival and growth, she has been known to make some tough, unpopular decisions. She's not exactly lovable. Many of the money-based institutions have been around for centuries and their cultural DNA and business narrative are forged inside every sinew and vein. That's why they can appear so slow to change. Conditioning and environment make everyone in banks, building societies, insurance companies, brokerage firms and other financial organisations think in a particular way, a way that often does not endear them to others. It comes across at times as old-school, reactionary, mired in custom and ritual.

After the worst global recession for 80 years people have stopped trusting financial services. In the past when dealing with retail, corporate or investment banking and so many other services that feed into the finance sector, the people that customers and clients were dealing with, from banker to advisor and from specialist to technician, were viewed as trusted commercial partners.

Before the 2008 recession the reputation of the financial specialist or the corporate or retail banker was based on the belief that their word was their bond, and that they would keep their promises, to the benefit of all. Although trust of financial services started to become less secure and heart-felt pre-recession it wasn't until the global financial crisis that trust in the financial services industry plummeted to an all-time low.

As the financial crisis took hold globally in 2008 in Asia Pacific many people reduced or liquidated investments and savings in order to hold more cash or to buy gold, luxury items (even jewels) and real estate. Anything rather than use a financial institution to look after their money. The US suffered a land-slide decline in trust and many markets, from housing to investment, were frozen for years and are only now starting to rebuild in an agonizingly slow manner. In the UK two banking groups, Lloyds TSB and RBS, had to be bailed out and RBS is still largely owned by the UK government today.

The Edelman Group is the world's largest PR organisation and undertakes an annual, global trust survey. In their 2014 global trust survey of 33,000 respondents 56% said they were familiar with banking and financial services scandals. Two-thirds of those surveyed reported trust in banking as below 50%, with trust in financial services at 48% (amongst the 'global, informed public'); this is almost the lowest level of trust when compared with every other global industry, with only the pharmaceutical industry at a lower level (32%). Countries in the EU have the lowest trust in their financial institutions with Germany and Ireland at 23% and the UK at 37% (up from 21% where it hit a new low in 2010), and with Asia Pacific (62%) having the most trust in their local financial services. Despite the country-based increases over the years, by 2014 financial services as an industry still have a long way to go to re-build trust. Worse still, newer financial services from insurance companies to credit card companies have also been negatively impacted by the general decline in trust. If it's a company that deals with your money the new rule of thumb is 'don't trust 'em!'[6]

---

[6] Based on Edelman's 'Trustbarometer' 2014 Annual Global Survey.

So much for the elderly lady on the bus, with the smart outfit and the most expensive handbag money can buy. Now let's look at the sulky, good-looking lad, sprawled out lazily in his seat, feet propped up on the seat in front. The levels of trust in technology are at the other end of the spectrum. In fact, the Edelman Trustbarometer places Technology as the most trusted industry globally, scoring 77% in 2013 and increasing by two percentage points to 79% in 2014. Technology, like my sulky teenager, is at the glamorous, good-looking and dynamic end of the market place.

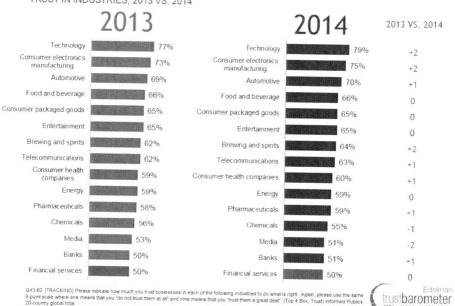

FINANCIAL SERVICES CONTINUES TO BE THE LEAST TRUSTED INDUSTRY GLOBALLY
TRUST IN INDUSTRIES, 2013 VS. 2014

	2013	2014	2013 VS. 2014
Technology	77%	79%	+2
Consumer electronics manufacturing	73%	75%	+2
Automotive	69%	70%	+1
Food and beverage	66%	66%	0
Consumer packaged goods	65%	65%	0
Entertainment	65%	65%	0
Brewing and spirits	62%	64%	+2
Telecommunications	62%	63%	+1
Consumer health companies	59%	60%	+1
Energy	59%	59%	0
Pharmaceuticals	58%	59%	+1
Chemicals	56%	55%	-1
Media	53%	51%	-2
Banks	50%	51%	+1
Financial services	50%	50%	0

Q43-60 [TRACKING] Please indicate how much you trust businesses in each of the following industries to do what is right. Again, please use the same 9-point scale where one means that you 'do not trust them at all' and nine means that you "trust them a great deal". (Top 4 Box, Trust) Informed Publics, 20-country global total.

Edelman
trustbarometer
2014 | ANNUAL GLOBAL STUDY

Source: Edelman. Used with permission.

But technology won't be the poster-child forever. In fact, its reputation has already been tarnished by the dot-com bubble of the late 90s and early 2000s. During this period internet companies were the darlings of the stock exchange which led to increased stock prices and market capitalization. Between 1991 and 2001 the bubble collapsed and some internet organisations failed or lost their previously high stock positions. Despite this, technology currently remains an exciting and rapidly-growing sector for investors. However, nothing stays the same. It's not only financial services that have a problem with trust. Globally, trust in financial services is only slightly lower than trust in business generally, as the Edelman report shows. Just because the financial services lady is old and the technology guy is a good-looking teenager, neither has the right to be complacent. When writing about the technology sector in 2014, Edelman noted that although technology and digital organisations are celebrated for their innovation, creativity and future focus, as they develop and expand, they may well fall into exactly the same kinds of business traps as the more established organisations such as those found in the financial services sector. As a small, agile business grows, it takes on a corporate structure and can easily fall foul of compliance, risk, legal, people and customer issues. And in the same way that technology has often led the pack in innovation, so too has it positioned itself as an industry which provides excellent people leadership and a great place to work. This may also be challenged as the industry matures. As Edelman puts it: *'The Trust Barometer darling for more than a decade, tech has established the trust and credibility needed to realize the license to lead through innovation, diverse and engaged employee populations and financial success. However, technology is now in a different league and therefore may face the greatest potential consequences for any failure to lead'.*[7]

---

[7] http://bit.ly/1KHTrph

In the world of the business everything changes. We all grow older; we all grow up. What was once in vogue becomes old-hat. The sexy, pretty boys and girls of the tech world will move from start-up to corporate giant as their industry develops and their bleeding-edge technologies move into the domain of everyday life. If they aren't careful in not too many years, they will look like, talk like and walk like the financial services sector, and run the very real risk of looking just as superior, arrogant and immovable. And untrustworthy. It's happening already. The all-powerful Apple computer company, once famous for its quirky and creative language is now coming across as a mammoth corporate giant in many of its legal and commercial operations and communications, with all the attendant challenges that brings. And there are also rumblings that its products are losing their edge. Watch this space. Nothing stays the same.

So there is no need for the good-looking teenager to scoff at the old-timer. In fact, it's useful to look at what they can learn from each other. What is it that each of them has done, said, believed or provided that has financial services near the bottom of the trust barometer, with technology at the top? And why does it matter?

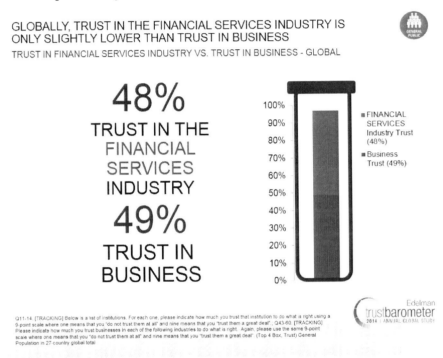

GLOBALLY, TRUST IN THE FINANCIAL SERVICES INDUSTRY IS
ONLY SLIGHTLY LOWER THAN TRUST IN BUSINESS
TRUST IN FINANCIAL SERVICES INDUSTRY VS. TRUST IN BUSINESS - GLOBAL

48%
TRUST IN THE
FINANCIAL
SERVICES
INDUSTRY
49%
TRUST IN
BUSINESS

- FINANCIAL SERVICES Industry Trust (48%)
- Business Trust (49%)

Q11-14. [TRACKING] Below is a list of institutions. For each one, please indicate how much you trust that institution to do what is right using a 9-point scale where one means that you "do not trust them at all" and nine means that you "trust them a great deal". Q43-60. [TRACKING] Please indicate how much you trust businesses in each of the following industries to do what is right. Again, please use the same 9-point scale where one means that you "do not trust them at all" and nine means that you "trust them a great deal" (Top 4 Box, Trust) General Population in 27-country global total

Edelman
trustbarometer
2014 | ANNUAL GLOBAL STUDY

Source: Edelman. Used with permission.

First of all, why does trust matter? Even at the lofty levels of the corporate world, we are humans first, and business people second. We hate doing business with people we don't trust. We love doing business with people we trust and connect with. Don't get me wrong, if you are the only company on the block selling melons and that's what I need I will buy from you, even if I hate you. But I won't enjoy the experience; I won't recommend you to anyone. I won't be loyal. And as soon as I can find another supplier, I'm off.

As Steven Covey, businessman, educator and author of *The Seven Habits of Highly Effective People* and *The Speed of Trust* puts it: 'When trust is low, in a company or in a relationship, it places a hidden "tax" on every transaction: every communication, every interaction, every strategy, every decision is taxed, bringing speed down and sending costs up. My experience is that significant distrust doubles the cost of doing business and triples the time it takes to get things done'.

Trust has two key components in the world of business, whether you are a good-looking teenager or an old lady. When I trust you I will trust in your competence and I will also trust in your willingness to do the right thing for me. I trust that a car manufacturer will sell me a car that is beautiful, high-performing and also safe and affordable. If I go to hospital I trust that the doctors and nurses know what they are doing and will look after me. I also trust that they will give me the right medication or medical intervention for my needs. Trust is all about me, me, me.

One major difference between trust in financial services and trust in the technology sector is that since the global crash people trust in the competence of banks, building societies and financial houses but they don't trust that they will use that competence to do the right thing for them. They worry that the financial sector is all about them, them, them and short-term financial and corporate targets, and not long-term, customer protection, support or growth.

However, for the techies people trust that they know what they are doing and they trust them to get on with it. That's why we get so shocked when there are dot-com bubbles that burst or when we hear that Google or Facebook have undertaken social research experiments by manipulating data. It's not what we expect.

And why do so many people love the techies? Probably because their industry represents creativity, innovation and the novelty and variety of something that is new, new, new. People like new. Humans are always looking for stimulus and the next fix of feel-good. That's how media, global communications and advertising have managed to get us to buy so much stuff. If we are getting a natural high that the feel-good of something new and special gives us we want it, and we want it now.

When I was a kid you could have plimsolls (the precursor to trainers) and you could have black ones or white ones. When my step-children were growing up there were a few more styles and designs but still, mostly black or white. Now you can have trainers that are designed in much the same way as a bespoke suit might be tailored for an individual; it's your own, unique brand of footwear. It will cost you a lot, of course, but what feel-good!

Business is more than trust. It's also about people and ideas and, of course, money. So what can the old lady and the sulky teenager learn from each other?

Here are just a few examples:

What can the young technology sector teach financial services?	Why is this important to the financial services sector?
A sense of creativity and innovation and a passion for trying new things. Everything is possible. Lesson: An ability to think and act creatively, the very life-blood of organisational growth and development.	Mature, well-established financial services often lack creativity across their organisation. The structure and process that keeps things organised and planned has a habit of slowing or even stalling innovation. Of course there have been pockets of hugely important innovation, such as Barclays setting up the first ever dedicated Behavioural Economics team in the world, a function specifically established to deal with the behavioural finance and economics side of investing and financial management. For the most part, however, many corporate financial organisations buy in their creativity.
A sense of personal pride, being connected with something that is new, innovative and leading-edge. Lesson: Feeling proud of what they are working for and with whom they are working. The pride is personally experienced.	People who work in the financial services sector tend to want to work for the company because of its products and services or its reputation or brand. It's not such a personal matter.

What can financial services teach the young technology sector?	Why is this important to the young technology sector?
A range of processes, procedures and systems. Everything has a proven method. Frameworks or functions and services that include HR, accounting, IT, management information, compliance, personnel, corporate communications, corporate and social citizenship etc. A lot of these elements might be considered boring but important. Lesson: A stable infrastructure provides a solid foundation for business growth.	Young techs often lack any structure at all. In the early years they are carried forward on a wave of passion and delight for their creativity and innovation. They are a tribe; all in it together. However, the larger and more successful they become, the more they require structure to manage and support employees consistently and fairly.
A sense of corporate pride, being connected with something that is powerful, historic and successful. Lesson: Feeling proud of where they work.	History is littered with young tech companies that lose a lot of their staff as they grow. That is because the employees are connected to the founders. It's a personal relationship that simply cannot be sustained when a 20-person company gets £40 million in investment and ends up having hundreds or even thousands of staff.

In my fifteen years of experience consulting, training and coaching I have found that the new leaders in these two sectors mirror the challenges faced and the good, and not so good, behaviours of all the other sectors. For example, financial services mirror the *grande dames* of heavy manufacturing and pharmaceuticals, which go back centuries. Any new sector, from bio to micro to nano, is a natural bed-fellow to the technology world. The larger the company, the bigger the brand, and the higher the revenue and the profits, the more training there is for knowledge and skills, for processes and systems. But as for new leadership? Behaviour, mind-set, attitude? That training often lags far behind.

Leadership is a well-oiled machine in financial organisations. There is a clear hierarchy. Leaders are given a remit and a strategy to implement. Go to it. But the bad news is that blindly following the leader because 'that's how we've always done it' has not protected our biggest corporates in all sectors from repeating unacceptable mistakes that not only fuelled recession but have blighted the lives and livelihoods of many innocent victims.

And as for the little guys in the digital and tech world they are fleet of foot and agile in action. However, as the start-ups grow the people who've been in it from the start will either get pushed out or get promoted. Unfortunately, all too often the good people leave when they should stay and some of the people being promoted because they are loyal and love the product or the founder, are not the ones that should be in these positions. They don't know how to lead. Worse still, they don't know how to lead as the company continues to develop and has to take on the corporate administration, bureaucracy and restraints of any successful organisation.

Leadership is not just a process or a skill. It's a way of being and doing with a little bit of having thrown in. (Source: *Fear of Freedom* by Eric Fromm: Fromm explains human identity as being a complex combination which includes doing [the things that we humans do], being [the experiences we have and what we make that mean] and having [the things and objects around us that we own, want, buy, exchange or use]). Of course some people are natural leaders, just like some people are natural artists or athletes. But for most of us, leadership has to be learned, experienced and added to the human DNA. And as for new leaders, if they want to be effective and successful quickly instead of uncertain, inept, intrusive or isolated or blindly following the same-old, same-old, they will have to learn to use 'The Code' for new leaders. Use 'The Code' and you'll hit the ground running as a new leader in record time. So why do we have to hit the ground running as leaders? What's the rush? And what's 'The Code' that new leaders need to use? In the following chapters this will be revealed.

Takeaways

1. After the global recession starting in 2008 trust in business is at an all-time low, with financial services almost the least trusted industry and technology companies the most trusted industry.

2. The 'old lady' of financial services and 'the young prince' of technology can learn from each other. Financial services can offer structure, process, procedure and consistency. Technology and digital companies can offer innovation, creativity, agility and new perspectives.

3. Financial organisations have well-oiled leadership machines but new leaders won't necessarily be successful if they follow blindly in the footsteps of previous leaders; that's what led to the worst global recession for eight decades. As technology companies grow from the tiny, agile tribe to the global conglomerate, they will need to develop a proper leadership structure and not simply a mind-set of follow the leaders simply because they are the founders.

Chapter 4

The first few days for a new leader: step up or cock up?

My first full-time job occurred when I was studying for my French and Italian degree. I worked in Lille in the Nord-Pas de Calais region of France for nine months. I was an *assistante d'anglais* in a secondary school called the *Lycée Louis Pasteur* (and nicknamed as L'Usine which means 'The Factory' because it had 2000 pupils). I worked with the kids going into the *baccalauréat* (the French equivalent for A-Levels or advanced GCSEs). At that time pupils who failed their 'bac' could, and did, retake it, sometimes twice. This meant that at the tender age of nineteen I was working with students who were often older than me. I was intimidated and terrified. Having met the four classes each containing thirty 'kids' (some of whom had beards) that I was going to be working with up to three times each week I was a nervous wreck. Even before my first, official day.

I was staying in a hovel but spent most of my weekends with a French family based in the countryside near Roubaix, a spit from the Belgian Border. With a brood of ten children the father of the family, Maurice, took me in hand and he gave me my first lesson about being in charge of my own destiny: he taught me about the benefits of planning and organisation.

On school days I had to walk two kilometres on a path alongside the railway line, cross the motorway flyover, catch two buses, one into Lille town centre and the other out again, and finally a one kilometre walk to the massive warehouse that was the *Lycée Louis Pasteur*. Maurice visited me the day before I started at the school and got me to do a 'dummy run' so that I knew exactly what to do and where to go the next day. He encouraged me to prepare my first lesson plan to be used as an introduction to the students. He also suggested that I lay out my clothes the night before so I knew exactly what I would wear if it was fine or if it rained. He also got me to organise a weekly carnet of tickets for the bus. He was such a patriarch that although I thought all of this was overkill I did what he asked. The whole thing was like a military operation and I was the only English assistant to arrive on time without copious sweating and even more copious apologies. One assistant never turned up at all. Although I don't think the buses were the problem, it could have been the students.

If you're just about to start work in a new leadership role I'm not suggesting that you need to do what I did the day before I had my first work-day at the Lycée although, it's not such a bad idea. If you don't know where you are going or what you are doing, people do notice the slight hesitation or the lack of confidence. I've known excellent new leaders who have taken quite unusual steps to prepare before starting work in their new leadership position and, like my first day of work as an English assistant, that means they look, sound and act ready.

There are different types of leader – so how do we define 'New Leader' here?

In 2001, a book called *The Leadership Pipeline* was a bestseller. It was written by Charan, Drotter and Noel, three distinguished corporate coaches and consultants who were connected with the General Electric Management Development Center at Crotonville, NY, USA. This ground-breaking book described the six levels of leadership for corporate leaders and the four levels for small to medium-sized enterprises (SMEs). Their models are often used today, with many organisations still using terms from their book, such as calling non-managers 'individual contributors'.

The Corporate Model - Large Business Organisation

Passage One: from managing oneself as an individual contributor without direct reports, to managing others.

Passage Two: managing managers.

Passage Three: becoming a functional manager – i.e. Head of Sales, HR, Operations etc.

Passage Four: becoming a Business Unit Manager – i.e. General Manager, VP, MD etc. heading up a single business within a larger entity.

Passage Five: becoming a Group Manager – i.e. CEO, President etc. heading up a group of businesses within a larger entity.

Passage Six: becoming an Enterprise Manager – i.e. CEO, Chairman etc. heading up the entire corporate entity.

The Small Business Model

Passage One: from managing self to managing others.

Passage Two: becoming a functional manager (the functional manager is usually absorbed by the manager of managers level for SMEs).

Passage Three: becoming a Business Manager (the group level does not apply here and the work of the enterprise manager is done by the business manager).

When I talk about a new leader I am talking about individuals who are already at passage two or three and they are moving up the ladder to passages three or four. I label them as a new leader because it is the first time they have moved away from the operational and tactical nature of business and now their leadership world includes the following ingredients:

- Their work is more strategic.
- They are no longer hands-on and do not actively participate in the operational or technical side of the organisation.
- They are managing direct reports who have teams who also have direct reports.
- They are in sole charge of tactical or strategic budgets and can make key financial decisions.
- They can hire and fire and re-structure teams.
- They will have regular connection and communication with the board of directors (other terms that are used for the executive team include C-Suite, Exco and Manco) or whatever the top-line executive enterprise or business leadership group calls itself is at the head of the organisation.
- They have meetings every day with key stakeholders.
- They are regularly called on to represent their organisation at conferences, exhibitions, seminars, presentations, media or press junkets etc.

You don't actually have to *be* ready or meet any of these leadership criteria. And actually, you *won't* be ready. It's not possible. Just *look* ready. What I'm suggesting is that you undertake some personal development and strategic action planning *before* you start in your new role or during the very first days of that role. It helps; it really does.

Why all this development and planning? Why can't you just rock up and do the stuff when you start in role? Because in a leadership role everyone is watching you.

One of the biggest mistakes that new leaders make is to think that they already know everything they need to know to lead successfully. They also often think that, at best, everyone is delighted to have them on board in the new role, or that at worst, everyone will give them a chance. In the cynical, high-pressure, results-oriented world of corporates even the most successful and enlightened organisation is full of people who will watch your every move like a hawk. They will judge what you do and what you say with the same vehemence and opinion that viewers reserve for talent shows like *The X Factor*.

Imagine it: You're watching the dowdy, frumpy, slightly overweight individual as he or she shuffles on to the stage to sing their song to *The X Factor* judges. You notice what they are wearing and you certainly don't like that. You notice that they seem over-confident, or nervous, and you don't like that either. Then you hear them sing and you think they're rubbish. Even more irritating is the fulsome round of applause they get from the audience and the polite, supportive comments from the judging panel which to your mind is clearly deaf and blind. Can't they hear? Can't they see? This person is crap. Worse still, your colleagues fall into a mixed bag of responses; some think the performer has potential. Others think they are fantastic. Some even agree with you.

That's what it's like for a new leader. Everyone is observing your every move as you saunter, amble or creep on to the stage that is their organisation. And they'll be judging you.

That's why you can't wait until day one of your new role. If you want to hit the ground running and make a difference to the people and the organisation around you in record time, you have to be as prepared for your job as the singers should be for that all important *X Factor* audition. You wouldn't expect them not to know the lines of their song, would you? And it's the same for you: do some planning and preparation *before* you start being the new leader.

Don't get me wrong, I'm not suggesting that a few days spent learning some leadership techniques and a few days of action planning will make you a perfect or even a successful leader. Although they might. What I am suggesting is that in order to be a successful new leader and in order to hit the ground running you need to step up at once. If you take too long to deliver the credibility, authority and effectiveness that today's new leaders *must* have, you'll be judged negatively. At best this will stall or slow your progress. At worst, it's a fatal error that could scupper your chances of real success in the role.

Far too often, I've seen really wonderful individuals being thrust into a new leadership role and given no support during those crucial first few days; days when the world is watching and judging. It's almost a life and death situation in metaphorical terms. In the same way that the emergency medical profession talks about 'the golden hour' so, the new leader has a golden week in which to hit the ground running, look effective and get the naysayers, doubters and hatchet men off their backs.

Perhaps you think I've over-reacting? Perhaps you think that that this first week of personal development and personal planning is a waste of time? Perhaps you are saying to yourself: 'Surely, as soon as I get into the role, my plans and ideas will change? I know I'm good. But I'm not a mind-reader! So why bother? Wait till I've had a few months in the role'.

Remember what John Lennon said: 'Life is what happens when you are busy making other plans'. I prefer the Eisenhower quote: '...plans are useless, but planning is indispensable '. Whilst it's true that strategies evolve, tactics change and plans get reviewed and updated, what usually changes is the look and feel of your master plan as you bed in to your new role. What doesn't need to change, and what can underpin that evolutionary master plan, is the act of planning; of gathering information, analysing data, organising your thoughts. This, in effect, is your planning.

I admit that sounds counter-intuitive. Planning is great, but plans get trashed. How does that work? Well, it's true but necessary. Ask anyone in sales. Ask anyone in the military.

What can leaders learn from successful sales people?

I've spent over half my working life selling products, services and ideas, or training and coaching people to do just that. In that time, things have changed a lot. We no longer sell products and services through a simple shopfront, with limited choice and a badly informed customer. We no longer get customers to buy from us simply because they like us or trust us. Today, most sales have a longer, slower, lead time, with highly sophisticated and informed buyers, who really don't care whether they like you and whose idea of loyalty is now distilled into a simple preference at the time of deciding to purchase. This means that sales people have to be constantly learning, unlearning and relearning, in order to find and use key information, and to create insights that are of interest and value to their customers. The most successful sales people have a game plan for identifying and qualifying their platinum leads, for developing value-based propositions that match client situations and for closing deals.

Here's what they are doing continually and consistently:

- Learning about their customer's world: their company, their industry and their competition by reading industry magazines, blogs, reports, conferences, news bulletins and from networking, talking to other people etc.

- Learning about their customer's issues: their strengths and weaknesses and their strategies and objectives by studying the PR output and the annual report and accounts etc.

- Using that learning to come up with strategic conclusions: the things that answer that 'so what' question for their potential clients.

- Using those strategic conclusions to come up with ideas and insights and value propositions that are targeted and relevant to the specific customer they are going after. These might be things that educate the client or that get the client to think about things in a different way. These conclusions don't all have to be perfectly formed or 100% accurate. They are there to get the conversation going, to progress the client discussion and to 'get in the game'. If information is a ball, you need the ball to play.

If you imagine yourself as a sales person selling *you* as the product then you'll do the same kind of continual and consistent learning when you start your role as a new leader.

- Learning about your internal customer's world, the people in the company where you are the new leader: the company's end-user or customer, their industry and their competition. If you already work in your organisation and have been promoted within it, this is still a good piece of revision homework for you to do, to work out where you all are now.

- Learning about the issues of your internal customer, their strengths and weaknesses and their strategies and objectives. Imagine you are an outsider to the organisation where you are about to be a new leader. If someone checks out the company what might they see? What are the winning formulas? What are the challenges that are being faced or will be faced in the near future?

- Using that learning to come up with strategic conclusions; the things that answer that 'so what' question for your internal customer. Imagine yourself standing before the entire organisation and saying 'Hi, I'm your new leader!' What you don't want is for them to say, 'So what?' You'd much prefer them to say, 'Great!'

- Using those strategic conclusions to come up with ideas and information and potential value propositions that are targeted and relevant to your internal customer. These form the basis of a vision that provides your new team with a direction to go in; and if you are thinking more strategically, your insights, ideas and the resultant vision can align to the organisational vision too. It's all useful data to get into the discussion and into the 'game'. Like sales people, you don't have to have all the answers. You can have lots of questions if you want. Many successful sales people deliver their personal insights based on their research and background planning. However, these same sales people will also ask good questions about the current and future state that could/will/does impact the client; and the client is all ears.

What new leaders can learn from successful sales people is that doing some homework is always useful. It gives you some data or some intellectual ammunition for getting into the game. If you rock up on day one with a puppy-dog, I'm-keen-to-learn attitude and without a voice-able opinion, many leaders will at best write you off. At worst, they will gleefully bring about your downfall. They may be able to do little more than trip you up, but even one early cock-up can take months to live down. Wouldn't it be better if you could just step up at once? Wouldn't it be better if you had some sort of vision, no matter how basic, that could get the discussion going as soon as possible?

What can leaders learn from successful military commanders?

Military commanders have always planned campaigns during times of crisis or war and have always developed some kind of positioning strategy before taking action. We've learned so much from the military that we use the words 'strategy' and 'strategic thinking' today in business yet these words come from military planning and their strategic conclusions.

The worlds of the military commander and the sales specialist are closer than you think. In his book, *Blink*, Malcolm Gladwell wrote about the US Military Games of 2002 known as the Millennium Challenge, which consisted of the enemy Red Team which was led by a rebel military commander in the Persian Gulf, a role played by former Marine and Lt. General, Paul Vann Riper. The US Pentagon fronted a Blue Team with the goal of using enormous amounts of data and information amassed from computers, satellites and sensors to monitor and predict the actions of the enemy. Whilst its information was highly accurate and useful for positioning and context it did not deal with the one thing that Van Riper as head of the Red Team knew all about, that war, like life in general and business in particular, is changeable and unpredictable.

Early on in the Millennium Challenge games Van Riper took action that was unexpected and unusual. Even though his team had the smaller force he went on the offensive on day one, sinking sixteen of Blue Team's most important ships in one attack. Blue Team, with all of their information, did not see it coming. Gladwell confirms that a good decision-maker is able to sift through information, analyse it and filter out the unimportant data. He says: 'If you get too caught up in the production of information, you drown in the data.' After this first offensive the Blue Team was allowed to reset the games and Van Riper was told he couldn't use his radar and that his missiles had been shot down. Blue Team subsequently won the war-games because Van Riper had to play by their rules and their narrative. Soon after the Millennium Challenge the Pentagon turned its attention to the real world, and Saddam Hussein, who did not play by its script at all.

What new leaders can learn from successful military planning is that the plan provides data and strategic conclusions. The plan provides any leader with a basic start-point. The plan allows you to get in the game. But military leaders also know that the real world is messier and less predictable; their planning is simply a foundation and a stepping stone and is likely to change. Being able to be proactive yet also flexible, adaptable and ready to change the game, is what all good leadership needs in order to be immediately effective.

Takeaways

1. In their book *The Leadership Pipeline*, Charan, Drotter and Noel describe six levels of leadership for corporate leaders and the four levels for small- to medium-sized enterprises (SMEs). This books deals with new leaders who are moving up the corporate ladder and moving from being a functional manager to becoming a senior executive, MD, CEO, VP, within either an organisation, business unit or group.

2. Such up-and coming leaders are no longer operational and will be dealing the senior team, (Exec.board, C-Suite etc.), as well as hiring and firing, setting strategy, dealing with tactical and strategic budgets and making key financial decisions.

3. For these new leaders the art of planning is everything and much can be learned from the world of both sales and the military. Learning from sales people means you will find out about your internal customer's world and issues and use your resulting strategic conclusions to develop your first pass at a work-in-progress strategy and a vision that get you 'into the game' as a new leader. Since the term 'strategic thinking' comes from military campaigns, learning from the military means understanding that business life is unpredictable and changeable and that planning provides data and a basic foundation for continuing to flex and update your vision and strategy as you bed into your new role.

4. A key point: everyone is watching you. Bear that in mind and you will take more measured and well-thought through steps during your first few days in role.

Chapter 5

Perfect DNA – the power of three

When I first starting working with Janie she had just won her third promotion in twelve months; she was delighted and terrified. When I heard the news and congratulated her she told me her first reaction was, 'Holy crap! What am I going to do now?' As it turned out she was told exactly what to do; to create a plan for a team re-structure plus a year-long strategy which she was asked to present to the executive board, two levels up, within the first two weeks of her new tenure. She might have been a bit confronted but she got on with the presentation. She also rehearsed it well; with a co-worker, with HR and with me. The problem was that it had everything in it. She had more slides and videos than a movie and whilst it looked and sounded great, the sheer size and scale of it were completely overwhelming: it was a turn-off.

When I met with Janie to go through this mammoth presentation she fought to keep everything in. It was all important; it was all necessary. So I took a different tack, asking her two seemingly similar, yet very different, questions.

Question 1: What is the message you think the Executive Committee want to get from you?

Her answers: 'Ideas for the re-structure, an outline strategic plan for them to discuss. Reassurance that my new team will do what we need them to do. Ideas on how business as usual will be carried out and also how the new strategies will be put in place. And finally, confirmation that the executive committee made the right decision to put me in the new role'.

Question 2: What is the message you want to transmit to the Executive Committee?

Her answers: 'Ideas of my own about what I can do to improve in our weak areas and maximise our strengths. Proof that I'm the right person for the role and proof that I can be left alone to do my own thing, whether that's strategy or BAU'.

Her own answers surprised her. Why were they somewhat different? Janie thought about this for a while and then confirmed her own findings: 'OK, the executive committee wants what they want and I want what I want. But in order to get what I want I have to give them what they want. And not only that, I have to make them look good and feel good about their decision and about my ideas, so that they will let me do what I want to do'.

After this discussion, Janie simply divided every element of her presentation into sections that answered her own needs and those of the executive committee. This helped her to jettison nice-to-have but unimportant topics and to include only the information that would deliver clear answers to the first question; with the sole aim of getting permission to have the answers she wanted to the second question.

That's what most leadership is about; even new leadership. It's only ever answering the two questions for anyone with whom you interact: what does this target audience want and what do you want? Often, you cannot get what you want if you don't give them what they want. It doesn't matter if it's your customers or your team members or your boss's boss. Give people more of what they want and you'll get more of what you want. It's a simple context, with only a few rules. Nothing you do should have long-term negative effects. In other words, the business must continue, without reduction in profits or revenue, and with no damage to the company's brand or reputation. In addition, no laws or regulations should be broken. No bad behaviour such as bullying, wilful blindness or favouritism should be permitted. No one should get sick or hurt, physically or emotionally, and no one should die.

That's not to say that as a new leader your life will be care-free, pain-free or hassle-free. You'll probably make people redundant, hire and fire, re-structure and re-vamp. You'll have people hating the changes you make and criticising your carefully thought-out plans. You'll face resentment, jealousy and small-mindedness. And, as long as you do your best to give your target audience what they want, within reason of course, you'll have much more chance of getting what you want; the freedom, the opportunity, the permission and the space to lead.

What new leadership is about is doing a deal, and that takes me right back to the war-games of the military and the craft of the sales person. Their worlds are always about deals; no one gets everything they want, not ever. It's all collaboration, compromise and collusion. No one ever won a war without casualties, uncomfortable political bargaining, or financial impact. The UK was virtually bankrupt after apparently being on the winning side after the Second World War and its economy took decades to recover. No one ever cuts a sales deal without giving something away unless they've got the only melon in the world or the unique item that no one else can copy, yet.

So being a new leader is about making a deal with a series of people. These include:

- The senior leadership who gave you the role in the first place.
- Your direct reports who have inherited you, whether they wanted to or not.
- The other leaders who are now on the same grade or rank as you and who may have a vested interested in your success or failure.
- Your external clients, customers, suppliers and stakeholders who don't give a toss who you are, they just want you to do something good for them. Remember it's all about them, them, them.

That's why I have developed an architecture that underpins this code for new leaders: it's the DNA behind 'The Code' that helps you to deliver more of what others want so that you get more of what you want and so that the deal is acceptable to both parties.

It's not a secret code, but more a set of principles and standards which can be divided into three categories: authenticity, attitude, and actions. In other words: who you are, what you think about, and the activities you engage in as a new leader.

Authenticity – being who you are

New leaders should be authentically themselves: I don't believe that leaders have to be a certain type. There are fantastic leaders who are extroverts, introverts, and ambiverts (moving between the two types according to situations and circumstances). What makes a new leader successful and able to hit the ground running is the fact that people see them as being genuine and sincere. If a new leader is seen as someone who has integrity, credibility and authenticity their true personality is accepted as it is. What is important here is for you to be you. It's good to be the best version of yourself that you can be; and you still need to be you. Don't copy your boss or your boss's boss. What they do and how they do it will not work for you in the same way that it has worked for them. If you emulate or mimic others, everyone will see the deception.

Do bear in mind however, that being authentic does not mean celebrating your uniqueness by allowing your bad habits, bad behaviour and bad attitudes to continue. If you are authentically being a pain in the arse or you are aggressive, rude or unhelpful, don't be surprised if you end up being a leader without a community, without a cause and without a clue! If you like some of the things that other people say and do, it's fine to use these; we can all learn from any good leader. However, make that action or that script your own and live it sincerely. Copying for copying's sake never works.

New leaders should know their own strengths and weaknesses: the best leaders are not actually the best leaders. They are not the best educated nor the most intelligent nor strategic nor clever. Some of the best ones have little education. Some of the best ones have so many weaknesses you could fill a book with their flaws. Look at Richard Branson or Steve Jobs. Both amazing leaders, chock-full of less-than-perfect attitudes, mind-sets and behaviours at times. The best leadership can be summed up by the Second World War pilots. The most highly trained pilots who flew by the rules and carried out text-book perfect sorties and raids were the first ones to die. That's because their very perfection made them easy to spot and easy to predict. The less competent, clumsy or imperfect flyers were the ones who had the greatest success, and lived to tell the tale. Which one would you rather be?

New leaders must see themselves as human and imperfect and must be prepared to confess that, in public: one thing a successful leader must learn very quickly is to stop bullshitting. As a very new leader a few months into her role, Janie asked her new boss, Howard, to review her personal business goals for the next six months. Howard was also relatively new in his senior post and was working until midnight every night. He forgot to read Janie's list of goals before his meeting with her one Friday morning. When Janie turned up instead of telling Janie that he had not had time to read through the goals he simply fluffed his way through the discussion and instantly lost any kind of credibility in Janie's eyes. So here's a quick tip. If you don't know something, admit to not knowing it. If you've not had time to read something don't bullshit and don't try to be the cleverest person in the room. Say something like, 'Janie, I'm really sorry, I haven't had enough time to read through this properly. Could you walk me through your goals now so that we can focus on each one?' Honesty, even about your weaknesses, is always well received.

Attitude - what you think about

New leaders will need to 'fake it 'til they make it': this principle does need some explanation.

It is *not* OK for you to pretend to be a rocket scientist if you're not. It is *not* OK to lie, cheat, steal, commit fraud or pretend to love something that you hate. People don't like that kind of faking and their internal 'authenticity-ometer' can detect it at once. It *is* OK for you develop the most positive mind-set that you can. And if you don't actually feel positive or confident and full of bomb-proof self-esteem and optimism, it is *absolutely* OK to fake it.

'Fake it 'til you make it' - you can change other people's perceptions and your own body chemistry by changing your body language

Amy J.C. Cuddy[8] is a social psychologist who is Associate Professor of Business Administration and a Hellman Faculty Fellow at Harvard Business School. In 2014 she was also named a 2014 Young Global Leader (YGL) by the World Economic Forum. Her ground-breaking research looks at how people judge and influence one another, particularly around two dimensions: warmth and trustworthiness (or how much other people can connect with us and like us) and competence and power (or how much other people look up to us and see us as powerful).

---

[8] http://bit.ly/1MWd2nu

One of her research findings indicates that if our body language is powerful and confident, even when we are faking it or doing 'power posing' as she calls it, we get really positive results. Firstly, we look, sound and act like a winner; the person you might hire, the person whom you see as a leader, the person you might agree to follow, even though they are new. Secondly, even when faking these power poses for as little as two minutes, before an interview, presentation or key meeting, Cuddy's research has indicated that our testosterone and cortisol levels change and we can often perform better even in stressful situations. Put simply, when you have a posture that makes you look confident and powerful, your brain appears to follow suit with the chemistry, allowing you to feel like that and be like that. If you stand powerfully, you look powerful and you are powerful.

When you 'fake it 'til you make it' you are still being your authentic self. The only thing you have added is some packaging or a uniform. This is normal. You package the message when you tell someone bad news; you are empathic, sympathetic and tactful. When you're at work you package your body with a working uniform; this might be a suit in the financial services world or it might be jeans and Converse trainers in the hi-tech world. And you might dress very differently in your own world. I have one suited-and-booted client who works in a bank during the week and never gets out of her jean shorts and hiking boots at the weekend. I have another client who, as MD, wears the T-shirt and jeans of his information services company only to be found in a tie-die kaftan on high days and holidays.

So if you are new to leadership and feeling the strain, do your 'fake it 'til you make it' power-posing *à la* Amy Cuddy. Stand up straight, make good eye contact and smile. Do this for two minutes every morning before going to work. When you are about to start a challenging meeting, conference call, or one-to-one, for the first two minutes do it again. You'll find that you feel more confident, more up-for-it and more together. This stuff works.

New leaders must see themselves as requiring on-going personal development and transformation. One of the best ways to get people to believe in you is to show that you have humility and vulnerability so that you come across as human, rather than untouchable and bomb-proof. If you can show that you are willing to learn and that you are still learning every day, others will want to connect with you. The bad news is that many leaders get on the rungs leading to the top of an organisation and stop learning; they think training and coaching are for others. New leaders who see themselves as the finished article will miss the fact that they can be a powerful instrument of inspiration if they act as a role model and are willing to continue to change and develop. The new leader may think that he or she can simply use what they have learned so far, as a formula for continued success. That's like getting into a sports car or a bus, after you've only ever driven an automatic Ford Fiesta; it's going to end in tears. As Marshall Goldsmith says in his book, *What Got You Here Won't Get You There*, you have to keep on learning as you climb up the ladder of leadership. There will always be something new. So lead the way in showing that you don't know it all and that you are still on your personal development journey. Even better, let people know what you have learned and thank sincerely those people who have helped you to learn. Let people know how your development is progressing. It sets a great example and encourages others to continue to learn too. Every time Rick attends a seminar, workshop or conference he always runs a follow-up, internal session with his direct reports, to tell them all about what he's just learned and how he will use that learning in future. These sessions always go down a storm. Makes such training cost-effective too.

The new leader must stop trying to be the expert and know-it-all; that time has passed: successful leaders have to let go of being the technical or subject-matter expert. As they climb the career ladder their leadership role will take them further and further away from the technical, operational and day-to-day activities of the very organisation they are leading. That has to happen. It's normal. As a leader, you no longer have the luxury of becoming or remaining the expert. Janie is an expert in debt but found that she was not an expert in credit. Worse still, within six months she started to lose her competitive and analytical edge on debt. That too is normal. It has to happen. If you want to remain the number one salesperson, stay in operational sales. If you want to remain the technician, stop leading others. Leadership takes you into financial, strategic, innovative and commercial worlds but it takes you away from your personal specialisms, expertise and killer skills. Suck it up. Let others be the experts. In fact, it's right and proper to support your direct reports and their teams and do everything you can to help them to be as expert, effective and high-performing as possible. You won't lose out. As long as you can find out what is going on when you need to, and as long as you employ or develop the best technicians and experts, they'll do the doing for you.

Actions – what you do

New leaders must be prepared to wear the uniform of the organisation. Imagine if you go to a school where the uniform is red and you turn up in blue. You stick out and you are not seen as 'one of us'. It's the same with leadership. In their book *The New Psychology of Leadership*, Reicher, Platow and Haslam confirm that those leaders who dress in a way that makes them look more like the people they are leading are more quickly accepted. For example, In the US in the early 2000s, George W. Bush with his leather jacket and cowboy hat was seen as a man of the people and as a regular guy; he gained badly-needed, early popularity. When leading Palestine, Yasser Arafat adopted the headscarf of the normal, rural population which showed that he identified with his people. Yes, leaders want to be authentic and real and themselves. But that will be around what they stand for and what they say. In order to gain early acceptance, if the uniform at your work is a dress with a jacket or a suit with a tie, then that's what you wear. If it's jeans and a T-shirt, then that's the uniform you adopt.

Once you have embedded into your new leadership role you might decide that changing the business 'uniform' is exactly what is required. However, for the initial, visual, first impression, lean forward and blend in. Don't worry; you can still be you. I recently coached a new leader who wore the relevant business suit, shirt and tie, and sported mismatched, brightly coloured socks. As for Rick, he always wears surfer jewellery beneath his suit. And, as for Janie's jewellery, if you look closely, you can see the tiny charm set she wears on her solid platinum necklace has a skull and crossbones on it. Enough said.

The new leader should have a cause or a vision for others to follow: if there is nothing for the rest of the organisation to get behind, or be 'inspired by', there will be no inspiration. And that's a pity. Every new leader wants to inspire. That's because inspirational leaders encourage followers and fans. Sounds better than a leader who leads through fear, doesn't it? But as a new leader, you may not have gained enough 'buy-in' to 'rock up' and inspire on day one. Instead, aim to develop a clear 'theme' for the board, the teams, the functions and all the employees or staff that you are going to be working with.

In times of crisis organisations often get behind a leader who is talking about the burning platform. In his book, *Leadership Transformed*, Peter Fuda also encourages leaders to have a 'burning ambition', a towards-strategy which is something positive for everyone to work towards and not just something to be scared of or to avoid. This positive goal is a more effective way to transform culture, maximise operations, process and system. It's a much better way to achieve anything that will ensure the on-going success of the business. And it's a quick and easy way to get your people behind you, even if you're brand new.

Even if you are not in a position to set strategy, you can develop a 'theme' which supports that strategy. For example, if the organisation's burning ambition is to achieve a double-digit increase in sales over the next twelve months, you could do worse than create a year-long project across all your functional, client-facing, non-client-facing and operational teams that encourages and rewards ideas and mini-campaigns for experimenting, for sharing ideas, for innovative sales activity etc. that work towards that strategy. One of my new leader clients ran a year-long, themed project to take one million pounds worth of cost out of the organisation. He asked every single function and department to get involved, from IT to marketing and from operations and admin to sales. He ensured that any idea taken up, big or small, was rewarded financially and also praised publicly and loudly. His company saved £2.6 million in 12 months. As long as your personal vision or 'theme' can connect at every level of the business unit or company you are leading, and as long as it's aligned to the business values and overall strategic aims, it will have legs.

The new leader has to have skin in the game: in order to be successful you need to have a sense of personal involvement, responsibility and accountability as a leader. You need to see yourself as having a personal role to play in the vision, strategy, communications and transformation of the organisation. Unfortunately, many leaders see others as being the individuals who will execute the ongoing 'delivery' of their strategy, whilst they remain in their office or connect with their external stakeholders or their next level up of line management. This means that they end up locked inside a virtual, or sometimes very real, ivory tower. Instead, new leaders can quickly win over hearts and minds by getting involved and getting their hands dirty.

When I used to work in the transport sector, early on in my coaching and consulting career, I found that the best new leaders learned how to drive a bus or a train or a truck. They connected with the accountants, the IT and the cleaners. They went out with the sales people and the drivers and the engineers. They found out about stuff and they showed an interest in how the plans and strategies of their organisation were playing out in the every-day world of everyone else. They had 'skin in the game'.

The new leader should communicate directly to key stakeholders: the most successful leaders will share key messages with their work-force and with other stakeholders, both internal and external. They act as the voice of their organisation and the brand. Such key messages might take place at conferences or seminars or internal team meetings, or one-to-one sessions. Wherever you have an opportunity.

The new leader must learn how to delegate: Rick has found this one really difficult. When we first started working together he confessed that since he is a specialist in the key software in his organisation and he knows more about it than anyone else he feels he cannot delegate its continued deployment to his head of department. The problem is that if you are a leader you have other things to do. There's no option here; you have to delegate. Worse still, you may be right; the person you delegate to may not be as good as you, but that is not the point. If you buy a dog you don't bark yourself. If you hire a chauffeur, you don't put them in the back seat and you don't back-seat drive. A good leader will learn to trust the expertise, skills and knowledge of their team members and be prepared to let go, and delegate. As long as your guys and gals are doing a good enough job, it's ok to delegate. They'll learn; they'll improve and they'll probably overtake your expertise, given time and support.

The new leader must learn to influence rather than dominate: it's all about questioning well, listening better and summarising like an expert. These are oldies but goodies. You have one mouth and two ears for a reason. And the best new leaders make every effort to develop the best questioning, listening and summarising skills. They ask probing, searching questions, encouraging people to open up and share their views. They listen carefully and fully, without interrupting, or trying to add too much value by giving all the answers. They learn how to summarise and play back what they have heard in order to show that they listened and understood and also to give them a chance to re-frame, re-position and influence what has been shared.

It's very important for leaders to learn and become expert in these three basics of questioning, listening and summarising; when they work, they provide the influencing fuel for discussions at all levels. Unfortunately, one of the biggest challenges faced by new leaders, by any leader, is that many people are too lazy, frightened or disconnected from their leadership and they simply don't tell them the truth. So that key information that you want to ask about, listen to and respond to never sees the light of day. Senior leaders find that their teams and direct reports will either tell the leader what they think the leader wants to hear, or they tell the leader whatever will get that big player off their backs.

Janie has found that she hears what is really going on when she takes her managers out for Friday evening drinks or when she buys her boss a coffee. She does this every other week and has found that 90 minutes in their company, with her questioning deeply, listening fully, playing back what she has heard with her own reframe and repositioning, tends to get her more usable data, intelligence and buy-in from her team members and her line managers than hours of in-house meetings. Of course, as a leader you can always pull rank but that's a card you play when you have to, not just because you can.

The new leader has a chance to aim for cultural development inside his/her organisation so they should go for it: truly effective leadership is where the leader aims to create a positive transformation in the culture of the organisation. Organisational culture is the glue that cements the ideology and the business narrative. However, it is often stuck in the past, and every newcomer succumbs to the best and worst of that culture over time, like 'The Borg'. In TV and movies about Star Trek, 'The Borg' force other species into their collective and connect them to 'the hive mind', in a form of assimilation. Avoid being 'Borg-like' and use your precious 'honeymoon' period to look at the current culture objectively. Think about what could be improved and start to talk about it. Don't change everything; it's neither necessary, nor your right to do so. But if you check out what is happening, really happening in the organisation, you'll soon find little bits of the culture that are less than useful or that have outlived their sell-by date. Make a note of these and think about role-modelling something that is positive, yet culturally different. And don't expect miracles. It's going to be one mind at a time. Cultural change takes time, but if you never start, you'll never change anything. And you might as well start on day one.

The remaining chapters in this book explain the six activities in the route map that forms 'The Code' for new leaders. Each chapter also relates in some way to the '3 As' or authenticity, attitude and action and how they help you to become an effective new leader at once. The chapters and the '3 As' don't represent that entire list of everything that you can do and say to be authentic, cultivate the right attitude and take the right action. Instead it is a list of the key things that you can do quickly and with immediate results to help you hit the ground running in days, not weeks or months. Read these chapters and you'll start being effective within your first few days.

Takeaways

1. 'The Code' for new leaders is a route map of activities that you undertake quickly and easily in order to unlock your immediate potential and be effective and look successful in the first few days of your role. Underpinning this code is a kind of three-pronged DNA which is a set of principles; your authenticity, your attitude and your action, or who you are, what you think about, and the activities you engage in as a new leader. These principles help you to be successful quickly as a leader.

2. Authenticity includes being the best you that you can be, being aware of your strengths and weaknesses, and seeing yourself as human and imperfect.

3. Attitude includes 'faking it 'til you make it' if necessary, seeing yourself as requiring ongoing personal development and transformation, and understanding that you cannot know or do everything. What this means is that you must empower others.

4. Actions include wearing the right 'uniform' for your organisation, having a cause or vision for others to follow, making sure you have 'skin in the game', showing others that you are personally involved and responsible, communicating directly to key stakeholders, and of course, learning how to delegate and influence rather than dominate.

5. Finally, a key action is working towards cultural change in your organisation, from day one as a new leader. Be patient; building something really good takes time – but you have to start somewhere.

Chapter 6

The doctor will see you now

When I was a kid I hated going to the doctor's. You had to go up to a bad-tempered receptionist who looked like she didn't give a damn and give your name. She would tell you where to sit and that is where you would sit. And sit. And sit. For hours. Unless you were an emergency. If you were an emergency you jumped straight to the head of the queue and got in to the next available doctor at once. That meant everyone else had to wait even longer. The doctor took his or her own sweet time with each patient, which could be five minutes, thirty minutes or two hours. And still we waited.

When I was little, people going to the doctor's surgery used to bring a thermos flask of tea with them. And sandwiches. Books and magazines to read; friends to chat with. Going to the doctor was a long haul.

Those days are gone; long gone. Today, the surgery or practice has a business-like receptionist who efficiently dispenses you at the right time to the appropriate nurse, doctor or locum. Depending on where you live, you may still feel like you are waiting to be seen for hours. But once you have reached the doctor's inner sanctum you usually get between seven minutes (standard) and ten minutes (luxury) with the doctor and you are out of the door before you've had a chance to ask all those niggling and potentially embarrassing questions that your internet search has raised.

In the modern world of business the doctor's surgery of the past and the present are examples of how not to deal with people. In the past, it all took too long and ate into precious time that, today, we can no longer afford. It's a pity; but nowadays we don't have much time any more to sit and wait or to sit and connect. In the present, with our never-ending lack of time our interactions are often too impersonal and we may not always get the individual and personalised attention we deserve. The seven minutes offered by the doctor in the new-style surgeries of today can mean that people's fears and concerns might not be dealt with until it's too late. Of course, the next phase of doctor-patient contact is likely to be on-line diagnosis in the home, so the gratification of personal attention will be even further delayed.

So why connect the concept of a doctor's surgery to becoming a successful new leader? You meet all types of people in a doctor's surgery. In your own organisation, perhaps even in your own team, you'll meet a cross-section of people and no one will be quite like you. It's a fallacy to assume that most people in financial services are analytical and lack creativity. It is wrong to assume that all IT people are introverted and geeky back-room boys and girls. Naturally, there are some cultural norms and shared characteristics; some people are drawn to the world of high finance or technology and information. But most people are their own, unique, imperfect, individual selves, with a life-time of hopes, fears, nurture and nature. Look in the mirror now; you'll definitely see a unique person staring back at you.

In a perfect world, the new leader would meet with a range of teams, both direct reports and wider teams, and connect with them on a personalised, one-to-one basis. They would follow the old-fashioned doctor's surgery model and everyone would be seen, one after the other, and given as much personal time and attention as required. Can you imagine that today? There simply isn't enough time. Business as usual takes over and you have to get on with your job. Now. Right now.

Chapter 7 deals with getting the best out of each key individual in your team and your wider set of stakeholders. One-to-one sessions allow that all-important, personal connection. But, boy oh boy, does that take time. If you want to hit the ground running in record time as a new leader, one-to-one sessions won't achieve that quickly enough.

So what about your immediate team or teams? How do you make that work, when individual agendas, burning ambitions and exploding platforms are all jockeying for position and demanding air-time?

Most new leaders are obliged to have team meetings, whether they are just joining a completely new company or are steadily climbing up the current company ladder. So that's just what they do. A week or two after taking up their role, the new leader calls a team meeting and aims to facilitate the 'new world'. It's never a pretty sight. A French leader once summed up UK and French meetings with new team members to me like this: 'In a UK team, the team members say *Yes* to the leader whilst they are in the meeting and then they go and do *No*. In France, that same team would argue with the new leader about everything and everyone, and the meeting would take hours. Then the team would leave the leader with a huge list of to dos and all the responsibility for everything. When you're a new leader, neither method is very satisfactory nor wins over hearts and minds.'

Question: How can you hit the ground running in days, yet win over your key team(s) quickly, especially when you don't have time to give everyone a one-to-one session that takes hours?

Answer: With a combination of MBWA and Team Surgeries. Be your own doctor!

So this is the first activity in 'The Code': winning over groups and teams.

MBWA – Managing By Walking About

In his play Henry V, Shakespeare had the young King Henry wandering amongst his troops on the night before the battle of Agincourt. Abraham Lincoln mingled informally with his Union Army troops in the early part of the American Civil War. These might be the earliest, recorded examples of MBWA. MBWA was a part of 'The HP Way' which was the open style of management pioneered by the two founders of HP, Bill Hewlett and Dave Packard. Many of the practices of The HP Way were widely copied by corporations throughout the United States and Europe in the late 1980s and early 1990s. Management gurus Tom Peters and Robert Waterman also wrote that wandering about in an organisation was the mark of an excellent leader. Most MBWA theory talks about the leader as taking a random journey around the business, ready to engage and talk to anyone and listening to everyone and everything. There are two benefits to the leader's MBWA:

1. To ask and answer questions and show, by connecting and communicating in an unplanned and impromptu fashion, that he or she is interested in everyone in the organisation or business unit.

2. To learn as much as possible about what might really be going on in the organisation; such information can be useful in managing current and future business and people challenges.

MBWA – Management By Walking About

MBWA might sound old and hackneyed to a new leader born in the 1980s but this is one of the 'old ways' that still works. No one likes a leader whom they suspect of being only interested in their own, ivory-tower view. No one likes a 'billy-no-mates' who refuses to connect. We are no longer in the world of the 1950s and 1960s, with white-collar workers sitting in enclosed offices with secretaries and assistants acting as guard-dogs so that they could avoid meeting with 'the work-force'; now that really was the old days.

So when should you do your MBWA? Whenever you can. If you get a chance to do some MBWA even before you start your new role, then grab that opportunity with both hands.

Whenever you get to do your MBWA, allow yourself the luxury of two hours at a time, and go where you are least expected. One leader I worked with in the financial services sector wandered into the head office and talked to the all receptionists and then all the PAs. She got so much out of those conversations that she wrote a report about it before she had even done one day in the new job. Another new leader in the technology sector went to his accounts department and really got his head around the financial dos and don'ts that help or hinder support for internal projects. Guess who never has a problem getting his financial compliance approved?

Don't be afraid to go anywhere, but do be prepared for people to turn you down. If they do, because they don't have the time, the inclination or they are just plain cynical, smile, say thank you and move on. Remember that you can always go back to MBWA when you are more embedded into your role. The earlier you can do it, the more likely you are to be experiencing the information without your own perceptions colouring it.

Ten years ago, I coached a new leader who had joined Barclays from Safeway Supermarkets. He was wearing chinos and a blazer and he told me, 'I'm an FMCG guy and I plan on bringing some new ideas to this old bank'. I tried not to laugh out loud in his face. Three months later he was in the same navy, pin-striped suit and white shirt as the rest of them and talking in the Barclays language, all his new ideas jettisoned. We are all impacted by the corporate culture we join and pretty soon if we want to survive and prosper we'll learn the language, wear the uniform and live the values of our new role. It will happen to you. So start during the honeymoon period, that special time when you are still the pre-new-role you, unchanged by any in-role filtering.

I don't know who said it first, but there is a real truism in the phrase, *distance kills information*. The further you are from the front line, the less likely you are to know exactly what is going on in your company. MBWA can reduce that challenge for you. Your front-line managers, shop-floor workers, salespeople, distribution partners, production workers, accountants, IT and systems specialists, and internal consultants are often working on a particular, specific yet vital part of the organisation where you are the new leader. They know stuff. They hear stuff. They want stuff. And it's part of your role to find out what that stuff is. It may not be all that important. But it's good to go to these people because they may have relevant knowledge about your products, services, industry, customers and environments that will help you hit the ground running. Pick your informant. The accounts department or the CFO will have useful data about costs and margins and earnings before interest and taxes (EBIT). The salesperson may know about a negative response from the market place to a particular product or service. Good to know.

Bear in mind that getting this useful knowledge often only works if you go to where these people are working. When you invite them to your office you change their environment and the message gets altered. Find them where they are. Find them in the places they like to frequent. Talk to them in their world and get the unfiltered ground truth.

Ground Truth

In her book *Fierce Conversations*, Susan Scott writes about 'ground truth'. In US military slang, 'ground truth' is used to describe the reality of what is really going on particularly during a tactical campaign or military manoeuvre on the front line, as opposed to what intelligence reports or plans say about what is going on. In other words, the ground truth is the real truth. This can happen in business too. The company reports and the press reports can say one thing. The individuals and teams working on the project or the task may have a very different version of events. In business terms, the new leader who gets to understand the ground truth is already ahead of the game.

Despite the fact that your view of the world will change as you bed in to your new role, it's important to undertake MBWA fairly regularly, maybe four times a year to begin with, because you'll get known as the leader who wants to find out stuff and who wants to connect. People speak in cynicism but live in hope; so even if some don't appear to take too kindly to your quarterly wanderings, know that they are often impressed and interested in the results of your journey. Undertake an MBWA as soon as you can when you become a new leader. It's urgent. It really is.

When you decide to do your own MBWA all you'll need is a script for introducing yourself. You can't just rock up and start observing, shadowing or asking questions without one. Here is a sample script:

'Good morning/good afternoon/good evening. I'm Rick/Janie. I've just become the (head of/ CEO/director/VP), and I want to learn as much as I can about different areas of the business. Would you mind if I spent a few minutes asking you some questions? And I'll be very happy to tell you what I'm doing and answer any of your questions if that helps. Would now be OK please?'

You know what they say, 'If you don't ask …!'

Remember that truly great new leaders will continue to undertake MBWA throughout their careers, even if this is only a few times a year. In the same way that we are all encouraged to meet with our key stakeholders, customers and clients on a regular basis, it's worth seeing your teams and the work-force at large, as also key to your success. Aim to continue to connect directly with people around the business, even if that is a global multi-national conglomerate. Become known for speaking in person to your teams and their teams and the wider teams of other functions and business units. If you do, not only will you come across as human, approachable and connected, but you'll find that you get plugged in to the 'real-world' of your business.

Team Surgeries

Team surgeries are a modern version of the doctor's surgery. Without the flask of tea and without the seven-to-ten minute slot.

Here's how they work:

- Get permission as soon as possible after starting in your new role, or even before you start your new role if at all possible, to come into the business and use a private meeting room.

- Set aside as much time as you can, at least two hours. And aim to run a series of these two-hour surgeries during your first few days as a new leader. If you can get permission to do this before you officially take up the new role, even better.

- Decide what you want to do during those hours. Most new leaders who run a team surgery divide it into sessions and time slots. For example, 9am to 10.00am might be a group session. 10.00am to 11.00am might be three lots of 20-minute sessions for an individual or small group of individuals to book a slot. Or the second hour could be an open forum for anyone to attend.

- Make sure you let your direct reports know that you want to run a team surgery so that they don't feel you are checking up on them or leaving them out. If you prefer, run the team surgery just for your direct reports and then once your direct team has got with the programme run another one for the wider team.

- Send an email round to anyone in your team or wider team to explain that you will be having an open-door meeting and to act as the official invitation to the surgery. Don't call it a surgery, people might think you are going to be using them as lab rats or cutting them open, taking blood samples or something; instead, call it a meeting, a kick-start meeting, a discussion etc. You can use the same type of wording as you would for the MBWA. In fact it's helpful if you do that since it makes you look consistent. All you need to do is explain what this open-door meeting is about. See some suggested wording below.

- Get to the room you've booked early. Be prepared to stay later than planned.

- Ask questions, answer questions and listen to the answers. This is live, in-the-moment stuff, so be flexible.

Sample Email: What is an Open-door Meeting?

It's a designated period of time which I want to allocate to anyone who wants to talk to me on 'x' date, between x am and x pm about anything to do with my role, my function, my team or the organisation and its products and services. There is no fixed agenda and you can book any of the slots in this email, either to attend an open discussion, or to book an appointment for a one-to-one. All discussions will be informal and confidential. I'm keen to learn. Will you help me please?

As for the content of the team surgery, if you feel that a truly open forum is too lacking in structure, then ask a number of questions to get the debate going in your email invitation such as:

- What is one thing that you think your team/company should stop, start or do differently?
- What works and what doesn't work in the company? Why is that?
- What do you think other people hate doing or love doing in the team? Why is that?
- What do you think customers, clients, suppliers or other external stakeholders feel or think of the company?

As with the MBWA you will do well as a new leader if you run such sessions a couple of times a year. Such informal discussions often reveal everything from deep-seated resentments to brilliant ideas. W. Edwards Deming was the American mathematician and statistician who is believed to have pioneered the theory of continuous improvement. He certainly helped Japanese manufacturing on the road to improved quality, increased production and better management after the Second World War. He wrote, 'If you wait for people to come to you, you'll only get small problems. You must go and find them. The big problems are where people don't realise they have one in the first place'.

So go and find these issues, get them out in the open and then you'll have a chance to deal with them.

Note that MBWA and team surgeries do not replace team meetings. They do not replace team-building activities or conferences or after-work drinks in the local bar. They are simply a mechanism for you, as a new leader, to learn more about the ground truth. They are also a good way for you to demonstrate to the new team which you are joining or inheriting that you give a damn about them as humans. It proves that you see your colleagues, team members and direct reports as more than just worker bees who will help the queen bee get all the honey.

It takes such a long time to get round everyone with a one-to-one session. It also takes ages to set up and get pay-back from regular team sessions. If you're in a hurry to hit the ground running, these two activities bring people and information to you.

Of course, once you are up and running in your role, you will organise one-to-one sessions and regular team meetings as agreed with your direct reports and with your wider team. These individual and team sessions will provide a more engaged, connected and honest exchange of information if you have undertaken your MBWA and team surgeries beforehand. It's likely that you will have learned something you didn't know before. It's certain that you'll get useful information and ideas from such sessions that you can play back and debate in future individual and team interactions.

As the leader you can have the last word, because you're the boss. But if you've already started to gain buy-in from the MBWA and team surgeries, it won't be such a big job to gain greater buy-in at the formal and more normal one-to-one's and team meetings.

The MBWA and the team surgeries make you look authentic, credible and willing to consult with the business. Even if you've already got your master plan and you know for sure that it won't change, letting people have a chance to give their view and to share their issues makes people feel valuable and significant. What they say matters. If you listen and pay attention to what you hear, you'll be consulting with the business, even if you can't give everyone exactly what they want. When people are consulted they end up feeling valued yet also responsible and those are good feelings to have.

The key point here is that people don't know or remember exactly what you said at these sessions but they do remember how the sessions made them feel. The MBWA and team surgeries are a way to make people feel good. Make people feel good and they'll return the favour.

Takeaways

1. As a leader two actions will help you to hit the ground running in days, and will win over your key team(s) quickly; these are MBWA, (management by walking about) and Team Surgeries. These are the first activity of the code. They are particularly useful when you don't have time to give everyone a one-to-one session. Such MBWA or surgery activities can be undertaken at the start or even before you start in your new leadership role.

2. Undertake MBWA by visiting key people where they are; don't ask them to come to you. Seeing and talking to people in their own function, department or business world will get you the ground truth, the real truth, of what is going on in the organisation.

3. Organise team surgeries by setting aside time in a meeting room and by inviting individuals and small groups, whether they come from your new direct reports or from your new, wider team, to come in and talk about what is important to them. What works or doesn't work; what they like or don't like. Their ideas for the future. It all helps you to learn about the people you are going to be leading.

Chapter 7

One mind at a time

In Chapter 6 you read about the actions you can take such as MBWA and team surgeries to start the process of winning over people by understanding both their issues and what's going on in their world. This chapter is more about winning over key individuals. One mind at a time. I know, I know, I'm imagining you throwing up your hands in horror and calling me stupid. You're going to tell me that you simply can't win over every mind, you've got 1,000 or 10,000 or 100,000 employees. But I'm not asking you to meet every single person, find out which sandwich they like and then buy it for them. It's a nice idea, but it takes far too long. And you don't have the luxury of time. If you want to hit the ground running in days, not weeks, you need to win the right people over, right now.

What I *am* suggesting is the second activity in the code: winning over some key people, one mind at a time. Key people are titular leaders, natural leaders or influencers. When they talk others listen. When they act others follow. These people may be amongst your direct reports, your wider teams, your peer colleagues or more senior line managers. If you've done your MBWA and your team surgeries, you will have worked out who a few of these significant movers and shakers might be. You won't have got everyone pegged; but you'll have a list of important individuals whom you can talk to and work with at once. And that's all you need to hit the ground running in days.

And you're also going to need this three-step plan of action. The three steps are Connect, Engage and Inspire:

- **Connect**: identify the right people to be talking to and get in touch with them.

- **Engage**: do what it takes to get them to pay attention to you.

- **Inspire**: use that connection and engagement to motivate people to give you a chance to prove you have some value to them, as quickly as possible.

Connect

One of the definitions of connecting is *bringing a person or people together with another person or people so that a real or notional link is established*. What this means is that you make contact with the right people, the movers and shakers, and then start the process of winning them over. So Step 1 is about connecting. And the very first person it's worth connecting with is your line manager or boss.

Your Boss

I was going to write a whole chapter about managing upwards and connecting with your boss and your boss's boss. Then I had a light-bulb moment. There are only a few things you need to do in order to make a connection with your boss or their line manager and win over his or her heart and mind. Read carefully.

Call, meet, email or message your line manager on a regular basis and tell them:

- what you are planning on doing;
- what you have done and how it went;
- what lessons you have learned that will inform what you are planning on doing.

This is wash, rinse, repeat at its most basic and perfect level.

Here's the thing; your boss is very busy and has her/his own objectives and to do list. What they need from you at the start of your new leader journey is reassurance that:

- They hired, selected or promoted the right person for the job.
- You know what you are doing, you are up to the job.
- You have a plan, an overview is fine.
- You have a process in place, so that they can get some idea of how you work.
- You will keep them informed so that they can keep other people informed.
- You will make them look good, or at least not make them look bad.

That's it.

And how do you do this?

Well, for a start, you need to meet with every one of your line managers or senior executives, whether dotted line or in a matrix, on a one-to-one basis if at all possible. You probably only need an hour with each; and I'm guessing that there will be around three key senior people you'll need to win over. So here's what you do with each one:

- Ask them what they need from you in your first ten to twenty days (ninety days is way too long). Make sure you play back to them what they tell you so that they know you've got it and understood it.

- Agree a regular and frequent level of contact, dates and times to be fixed. This doesn't stop you connecting with each other at any other time. But setting fixed dates and times for regular updates is reassuring for your senior leaders and it's a good habit for you; deadlines give you a framework for taking action.
- Agree what content that each of these three people wants to receive from you as an update.

It's all about developing the muscle of connecting regularly with your boss, or senior line managers, perhaps with a brief email or a brief phone call. Rick agreed to email his bosses every Wednesday and Friday around 4pm since he discovered that this gave them enough feel-good to give them a good week and an even better weekend. Rick was based in the UK with two bosses, one in London and one in New York, so he would speak to one every Monday morning (8am GMT) and the other at 1pm that same day (8am EST).

If you have two bosses, more common in our global economy than could have been imagined even five years ago, then treat them both in the same way. Wash, rinse, repeat.

As for how much you write or what you talk about in your update, make it short and sweet. When Rick first started in his new role, I got him to meet with his UK line manager on day one and to telephone his US line manager on day two, to agree what was required. Here is a sample email from Rick's archive, written after only two days in his new leadership role:

Hi XXX,

Please note my planned activity, achievements so far and lessons learned:

Planned activity*: Two team surgeries with the Ops team heads to assess progress on green initiatives and current obstacles on the Go Green project.*

- *Strategic planning session with CFO on understanding the cost-base for project Tijuana.*
- *Creation of final team surgery report with strategic conclusions.*
- *Development of gap analysis in sales and marketing plan so far, meeting the CMO on Wednesday at 10am to look at Q4.*

Achievements so far*:*

- *Timing and location of team surgeries for all other departments finalised.*
- *New Exec PA briefed and working practices agreed, he will send this report to you tomorrow by close of play.*
- *Team surgery report half completed, still awaiting Ops team report, deadline tomorrow at 5pm GMT.*

Lessons learned*:*

- *We need to improve diary/Outlook management across exec PA's, this can be done through my PA, acting as a project lead for all the other board PAs.*
- *Team surgeries need to have the time allocated more tightly to avoid over-runs. My PA will message me when deadline is reached for each one*
- *Sales and marketing have key strengths in three of the quadrants discussed, but there is a potential weakness in quadrant four, this will require further investigation, planned for 17th June at 4pm, peer review meeting.*

My next follow up will be sent to you on x date. Thanks

That's it. Make sure that your boss, or your boss's boss, or whomever it is that is more senior than you and wants in on the communications trail, receives regular, informal yet structured updates. Keep connecting with them. You'll be surprised at how much you can keep them off your back.

Your Direct Reports

Look at your direct report team and divide each individual into 'leaders' and 'followers'. It is possible that within days of starting as a new leader the team 'leaders' become clear to you. They may or may not actually be a team leader in terms of their job description. They might be a natural leader, someone who has the personality, or the personal power, the charisma, flair and charm to lead others. They could be an influencer of others, someone who can convince or persuade others to act or not to act. They could be a technical expert or specialist who has earned the right to lead others in his or her chosen field. Whatever reason someone comes across as a 'leader', you need to win them over, and fast. These are the people you will meet with first because they have the most power and influence. What they say and how they react to you can help or hinder your early leadership days and be the difference between success and failure. These guys can literally bring you down.

If you think it might be difficult to work out who these 'leaders' and 'followers' actually are, then use the Direct Report Matrix of power/influence versus potential impact. Take the names of all the people whom you think might be important and plot them into a descending order of power and influence versus how much impact your role might have on them. When you have plotted all the names on this matrix you should be able to see which people are the ones that need your attention at once. It may not be entirely accurate and scientific, but it's a start. You can always re-plot these people if things change.

Example of completed Direct Report Matrix of power/influence versus your potential impact:

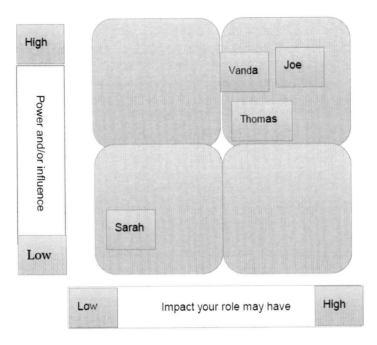

Once you have been able to identify these 'leaders' and you have met with them, you will start to see a pattern of the challenges faced. You will also see the things that are working well, oiling the wheels of the working environment. So this information will provide you with a useful map of the areas you can leave well alone, at least for a few months, and the issues that need to be tackled as soon as possible.

You will then need to meet with the 'followers'. These people are perhaps not the natural 'leaders', or they are too new in role to think about leading. It is also important to know what the followers are doing, thinking, feeling and saying. However, you do have more time to win over these people, quite simply because they are not the key movers and shakers. They will follow what others suggest, including you, at least during the early weeks and months of your tenure as their leader. Your MBWA and your team surgeries will reveal their views and concerns.

Once you have singled out the key people, methodically work through each one, using the following model. And do it with urgency. Aim to meet with every one of your direct reports within the first three days of your new role, even if this means you spend only 30 minutes with each and you are in back-to-back meetings. If you are not exhausted at the end of each day during your first few weeks in the new leadership role, then the chances are that you are not being a successful leader. These crucial one-to-one meetings send the message that your direct reports are important to you. Remember that you will also be doing your MBWA and running team surgeries, so you are going to be doing a lot of connecting.

Engage

There are many definitions of engage or engagement. But the one everyone at work always talks about is around 'employee engagement'. Employee engagement can be summed up as 'a workplace approach designed to ensure that employees are committed to their organisation's goals and values, motivated to contribute to organisational success, and also that they develop and maintain their own sense of well-being and motivation'. So that's easy then!

Actually, it's not that hard. Most people fall into the trap of thinking that engaging with employees is about a carefully planned, beautifully executed series of messages. It isn't. A big mistake you can make as a new leader is to hold back until everything is sorted and every message is crafted and well-honed before engaging. Remember JB in the foreword? Don't wait. As soon as you are in your new role, you already know that everyone is watching you. Do something and do it now. It's about acting quickly. Here's the why and the what.

The *why*

You need to act quickly because in our over-crowded, noisy world where no one has any time any more, people won't focus on you for long before making up their minds about you, rightly or wrongly, and moving on to something more interesting or potentially more lucrative. If you don't act quickly, most people will simply stop being interested in you, and they will turn their attention to someone and something else. As for the people who are directly affected, influenced or impacted by you, they will be watching you like a hawk, waiting for you to succeed or to cock up. It's in our human nature to judge so we don't need to beat ourselves up for having less than empathic feelings about our fellow leaders. In the same way that a cat will instantaneously judge a jump up onto your lap, your fellow work-colleagues judge your performance. They need to know if you are friend or foe, strong or weak, supportive or destructive, professional or a 'plonker'. The judgements are going to go on whether you take any action or not. So if you act quickly and decisively, you'll catch the attention of most people and send out the message that you're the real deal.

You also need to act quickly because we humans are an imperfect lot. We fill in the blanks and will literally make up any information that we don't have in order to avoid having those blanks. Our brains do that all the time to help us plough through the millions of bits-per-second of information that are constantly bombarding us through our senses. So if you don't want other humans to take one look at your slow reactions and make that mean that you are weak, then say or do something that gives their brains something to work on. Start talking and start taking action.

To begin with, tell them what you want them to know about you or they start inventing information about you. Because Janie delayed starting her team surgeries until a week into her new leader's role, she discovered that most of her direct reports thought she was either a stuck-up cow or an introvert who was in way over her head. Neither, by the way, is true. She is actually a reflective, careful and very professional individual. In the eyes of her peers, line managers and direct reports, Janie was perceived as slow because they thought she was unsure and afraid. It took her weeks to get over that initial, negative perception.

You need to act quickly because first impressions count. First impressions are often lasting ones. If the first impressions you create with your direct reports are that you are authentic, sociable, willing to connect and able to move quickly and decisively, all those watching you will think that you are a good leader.

The *what*

The MBWA and team surgeries help to create a sense of employee engagement very early on. The one-to-one, one-mind-at-a-time sessions are also useful for creating this engagement at a more tactical level. Therefore, at each one-to-one meeting, make sure you follow a basic plan.

- Thank the person for meeting with you.

- Tell them how long the meeting will be and stick rigidly to the timing.

- Promise them that this is the first of many such meetings and that each one is confidential.

- Explain the purpose of the meeting, for example: 'To get to know you and find out what you do, how you do it and what I need to learn in order to understand and support your role'.

- Explain that this meeting is about you being in learning mode. Explain that you are new and you know that there are huge gaps in your knowledge and skills and experience. Be honest about this. Don't say you are crap at everything if you are not. But if there is a weakness, or a lack of understanding, then admit to this. Janie won huge points with one of her key direct reports when she explained that she knew everything about debt since this was an area where she had specialised, but she also added that she had patchy knowledge about some areas of credit. This transparency simply elevated her in the eyes of her colleagues and direct reports who were quick to recommend a subject matter expert that Janie could talk to about credit.

- During the conversation, make sure you speak no more than 30% of the time and listen attentively for the remaining 70%. When the direct report has answered your questions and been encouraged to talk about themselves, answer their questions. Be ready with your potted history. And if you don't know any answers, admit to that, agree to get the answer by x deadline and then make sure you hit the deadline with the required information.

The *how*

If this book was about communication skills I would be talking a lot about body language, non-verbal cues and key language patterns. But actually, what is really important here is the fact that you hold the session at all. If you have wonderful communications abilities, so much the better. But even if you are shy, quiet and geeky, or you are introverted with a stammer and believe that communication skills are not your forte, you can still have a massive and positive impact on your target individuals. Being straight and open gains more points than someone who has a glossy presentation and marvellous communication skills, but no substance or authenticity. Just be yourself. Do it your way. Your 'audience' will know whether you are telling the truth and how genuine you are. Simply bothering to hold a conversation at all and being ready to learn will prove your authenticity and your potential as an effective leader.

However, there are some key techniques that anyone can learn and use, whatever your personality or communication preferences; and you can use these techniques with groups or with individuals. Your call.

Technique 1: *Thinking Out Loud*

Thinking out loud means that you say what you are thinking. And you reveal what you are thinking and feeling. Of course you need to make sure that what you say is relevant, about work and is appropriate. You cannot say, 'I think you are fat and ugly and an axe murderer'. What you *can* say is that you are still learning, or working out a strategy, or aiming to make improvements. Use this technique when someone says something you don't understand or find difficult: you'll come across as sincere and human. You can say, 'So here's what I'm thinking right now. I'm thinking that this sounds quite a difficult and complicated process. Can you take me through this in a little more detail, please?' Or, 'I'm sorry, I don't really understand what you are saying: can you just explain what you mean by *x*?' Or, 'I'm a specialist in debt rather than credit, so I'm wondering if you could just tell me more about how that would work in this situation?'

It is a leadership strength to admit weaknesses and to show that you are willing to be a little vulnerable and to continue to learn. It is a leadership strength to show your 'work-in-progress' thinking. When you think out loud you are sharing your thinking and not your conclusions. In fact, thinking out loud is one of the quickest ways to engage other people. And if someone comes across as aggressive or negative, you can say something like, 'Actually, how you are talking right now is coming across to me as a bit aggressive or negative. Is that just the way I am perceiving this, or is something upsetting you?' Most of us *don't* think out loud. What we share are our carefully packaged conclusions. When you learn to use this technique you will find that you connect very powerfully with everyone. You will get their attention in a way that is positive and shows emotional intelligence.

Thinking out loud is also useful when running any meeting or one-to-one. It allows you to keep people engaged and listening, as you share with them your reflective journey, what you are thinking right now and what is going on inside your head.

Thinking out loud can also improve a difficult situation. When a senior VP of marketing had received some 360 feedback from her direct reports that, to them it looked as if she was favouring some over others, she decided to use this technique at her very next team meeting. She started off the team meeting by talking about the results and giving her views on them; how surprised and upset she was to hear what others thought of her. She added her thoughts and ideas for connecting with the key people that others saw as favourites and explained why certain projects they were working on had demanded her attention. She explained that she had not realised how this looked and never had any intention to favour any one person in her team over another. She ended by asking what she could do to ensure that no further favouritism could be perceived. The team members loved her thinking out loud, and new actions were put in place around updates and meetings to avoid any future concerns. Not only were her words well received, but she also managed to improve harmony in the team and their subsequent performance increased by 30% in one single quarter.

Technique 2: *Asking, 'How do you feel?'*

Often we talk about how people think but that is quite an intellectual construct. It's important to know what emotions are going on *behind* the professional and more formal façade. By all means, ask each direct report what they think about *x*, *y* and *z*. But more importantly, make sure you ask them, 'How do you feel about this decision?' This question asks their brain to connect with their internal emotional responses. This simple question can often reveal even more information. The late Maya Angelou said, 'I've learned that people will forget what you said, people will forget what you did, but people will never forget how you made them feel'. This is so true. Make people feel good and they won't remember that your tie had ketchup on it or that you are weak at credit or that you stuttered a little at the start of the meeting. They *will* remember that the meeting made them feel positive, hopeful, included and valued.

Technique 3: *Doing a 'Brain Dump'*

Immediately after every initial one-to-one session do a 'brain dump'. This is where you spend a few moments in quiet reflection and note down, not just what you said and what others said, but how you *felt* about the conversation. Did you feel that this person was telling you the truth? Did they come across as *glad*, *sad*, *bad*, *mad*, or something else?

In other words, what I'm asking you to do is think beneath the surface of the conversation and capture your impressions of it. What was *really* going on? What was *not* being said that you inferred or guessed? It's all about the subconscious response.

If you read *Blink* by Malcolm Gladwell, you'll see that the nervous system and the unconscious mind respond with lightning speed to an individual or a situation, and the conscious mind takes a lot longer to catch up and make sense of it. So the quiet reflection is a way to look into the sensed responses and reactions that your day-to-day mind has consigned to the deeper recesses of your brain. But you *must* do this brain dump within *five minutes* of the end of the conversation. Otherwise, your brain will get side-tracked with other, external stimuli and influences, such as your emails, a phone call, your next appointment etc. Trust me, this works. And everyone can do it. Write down what comes up for you and you'll be surprised at how relevant, meaningful and detailed this brain dump information can be.

In order to do this take five minutes alone and think about what you have just experienced in the one-to-one. Make notes about what comes up for you. If you are a mind-mapper put the person's name at the centre of your page and have the usual mind-mapping strands coming off it. If you are a linear, list-maker, just write down bullet points of your impressions. And if you are really struggling to get some time alone, go to the loo. No one is going to stop you locking yourself into a cubicle for a few minutes and they don't know you are just sitting there on the closed toilet seat, thinking and making notes. Speed and quiet are essential for a good brain dump.

Play your 'Get out of jail free' card

This is a technique to use when things don't go well. No one is perfect and mistakes and cock-ups can occur. So let's imagine that you have had a one-to-one with someone you really wanted to engage with and it didn't go well. Perhaps you forget to ask some key questions; perhaps the person was a bit closed and unresponsive. No problem, all is not lost. Use your 'Get out of jail free' card. It's an imaginary card, based on the game of Monopoly. In Monopoly, if you land on the 'Go to jail' position on the board and you have the 'Get out of jail free' card, you can stay out of prison and just keep going round the board. It's the same with my imaginary card. After the meeting is over, write a note or email to the person in question. Start with, 'Thanks for x meeting today; I found it really useful and you really made me think. And here is what I have been thinking...' Then you can say all the things that you wanted to say in the meeting, or all the things that you have thought of since the meeting ended. A bad meeting is simply an opportunity to re-think, re-work and re-set; the game of work continues. All is not lost. It rarely is.

Technique 5: *Getting into the Feedback Loop*

Feedback is the foundation of all successful business people. From the moment you hit the ground as a new leader, seek out regular feedback. When you engage with the people you have identified as important and influential, ask them to tell you what is working for them or what is missing. Ask them how you can do things better. Keep asking. Make it a deep-seated habit. And give regular feedback too. Let people know how they are doing and very specifically take every opportunity to catch them doing things right so that you can praise them for it, loudly and publicly. The field of positive psychology has demonstrated that when people are praised for a positive achievement, they will repeat it, time and time again. So get into the feedback loop and wherever possible and appropriate make it a positive loop, and watch the good behaviours, attitudes and actions continue.

Inspire

The definitions of inspiration include the following:

- The process of being mentally stimulated to do or feel something, and especially to do something creative.
- A sudden, brilliant and timely idea.

I like both these definitions. As a new leader, one of the best ways to hit the ground running in days and not weeks is to come up with a sudden, brilliant and timely idea, or to encourage someone else to think or do something that is creative, innovative or new.

When you inspire someone, you motivate them and you give them a sense of positive energy, hope and forward-movement; in fact, a whole bunch of things. Inspiring someone is not about being the best and most charismatic speaker or presenter. You don't even have to be the best leader. You just need to pay attention to your surroundings and listen carefully to what the key people you meet with are saying to you. When you do that you will automatically pick up clues and signals for what things will inspire others. Bear in mind that you are not trying to win over every single heart and mind, just the hearts and minds of the key people who can make or break your first few days in your new role.

So what inspires other people?

- **They have to believe you**. If you are using the techniques outlined above, they will make you look and sound human and emotionally intelligent. If you sound human and even humble, people will be drawn to believing in you and your initial plans.

- **They have to like you**. No one likes a smart-arse. No one likes over-confidence or arrogance. Sharing your 'potted history' and showing that you are not an expert at everything and asking for people's views so that you can learn are all techniques for winning people over and getting them to like you.

- **They love a quick win**. Even in the world of work, which is serious and about making money and having success, people love a quick win. It's motivational and positive and it provides a sense of dynamism and hope. So look for quick wins where you can move the game forward.

Having listened to one particular individual during a key one-to-one session, Janie discovered that her team leader wanted an iPad. He didn't need one; he just wanted one and he had noticed that other leaders in peer teams had iPads for the mobile work they were doing and he wanted to have one as well. Janie checked with HR and procurement and discovered that some left-over, new, yet unused iPads were available in the organisation. She simply requisitioned one and gave it to the team manager. He was over the moon and has been her staunch supporter ever since. It cost her about £600 out of her budget.

Sometimes it is the simplest things that inspire people's confidence and loyalty. This guy felt heard and valued, both as an individual contributor and a human being. It was a tiny price to pay for someone feeling good about themselves and their new leader. Of course, other quick wins might be psychological, such as encouraging a person to manage a project with good visibility, or arranging for a direct report to have a mentoring session with a senior leader. Whatever you decide to do to inspire others, it doesn't have to be around giving a rousing speech or doing a five-minute, comedy stand-up routine, unless, of course, you are really good at those things. In which case, go for it! What is important here is to put yourself in the other person's shoes and aim to inspire them in a way that is individual and personal to them.

When you want to win over one mind at a time, especially at the start of your new leadership role, you don't have to do very much. In fact, being a newbie, you probably can't do a lot to begin with. That's OK. Remember, all you are doing is building early connection, engagement and inspiration, so that these key people will give you the time and space to learn how to do your job properly. Instead of being neutral or detractors, they will be positive advocates who tell anyone who will listen that you are a really great leader. Job done.

Takeaways

1. As a new leader it's vital to win over as many people as you can, one mind at a time. You can do this by undertaking the second activity in the code. It includes a range of actions and steps and it can be summed up with three actions; connect, engage and inspire.

2. **Connect**: identify the right people to be talking to and get in touch with them.

3. **Engage**: do what it takes to get them to pay attention to you.

4. **Inspire**: use that connection and engagement to motivate people to give you a chance to prove you have some value to them, as quickly as possible.

5. Plot all the key people who are your direct reports into a matrix of power/influence versus the impact your role might have on them. It won't be perfect but it will be a starting point for deciding which people to talk to first. Start with the 'leaders' asap and then move to the 'followers'

6. Use a range of techniques to help you win over each person including: *Thinking Out Loud*; *Asking, 'How do you feel?'*; *Doing a 'Brain Dump'*; and *Getting into the Feedback Loop*.

Chapter 8

Get good at thinking

I'm old enough to have had a number of careers across my twenty plus years in business. I started as an Import/Export Executive and moved up to Import/Export Manager. I've been a National Accounts Manager and an International Accounts Manager. I've worked at Pinewood Studios, home of the James Bond movies and I've made business television. I've been a voice-over artist, a script-writer and story-boarder for audio communications and training, e-learning, self-paced learning, webinars and games. I got into learning and development at thirty-six and had to go back to school; that was tough, especially with most of my fellow students being a lot younger. But by the time I had finished my HR diploma and my coaching certificate I realised I had something they didn't have; the ability to think critically.

Some pundits say that critical thinking is an invention of modern education systems. I think it's more likely that in Ancient Greece, when Socrates was coming up with all his fantastic philosophies, being able to think in a big picture, reflective, focused, analytical, logical, unemotional and disciplined manner which will lead to strategic decisions and actions, was both an art form and something on the personal agenda of every learned person. I don't suppose for one moment that Socrates realised his pronouncements would be around thousands of years later. Here are some of his oldies-but-goodies:

The only true wisdom is in knowing you know nothing

The unexamined life is not worth living

The way to gain a good reputation is to endeavour to be what you desire to appear

Let him that would move the world first move himself

Critical Thinking

> ### Definition
>
> Critical thinking is the study of clear and unclear thinking. The US National Council for Excellence in Critical Thinking defines critical thinking as 'The intellectually disciplined process of actively and skillfully conceptualizing, applying, analyzing, synthesizing, and/or evaluating information gathered from, or generated by, observation, experience, reflection, reasoning, or communication, as a guide to belief and action.' Some dictionaries give the meaning of the term critical as being 'crucial.' Others give it the meaning of 'discerning judgement'.

Whenever I bring up the subject of critical thinking for the first time to new leaders they throw me a scornful look. It speaks volumes. It says: 'Are you mad? I do critical thinking all day every day, I don't need to learn how to do it'. But actually most of them are wrong. They don't do critical thinking at all. They do 'operational' thinking.

Most new leaders have come up the ranks through more junior levels of management and they have managed people and tasks. They may even have led projects; been the number one, go-to specialist for a function or an activity or a department. But they are still managing. Managers often have operational thinking; their thinking is all about what to do and how to do it. As a manager, no one asks you to come up with a strategy for the future of the business. They ask you to come up with ideas, but it's tactical at best, developed specifically to deal with an immediate challenge, often with a deadline, like a marketing campaign or a sales target. Managers have to work out ways to execute and implement something. Managers problem-solve and create solutions. Managers work in the business on the front-line, at the coal-face, in its guts.

Leaders have to do something different. They need to do strategic thinking. They need to be able to do more than solve a problem or decide what is needed as the very next step. Strategic thinking is about being future-focused. Leaders need to ask some of the bigger, more ethereal and uncertain questions than operational managers. They need to be asking ambiguous, complex questions which don't have easy answers. What if? What's next and why? Who's worth it and who isn't? Who do we need? Why bother? Why change? Why not? Why now? They need to be able to work on the business. They need to be able to step outside of the day-to-day, deadline-driven, results-oriented grind of To Do lists. They need to think about what comes in the next six months or the next financial year, or in one year or even three to five years. They need to think about what might happen, what has to happen and what must not happen, and work out what all of that means. They need to avoid operational thinking and fixed assumptions. They need to ignore personal feelings of discomfort and challenge around tough decisions or challenging plans.

So this is the third activity of the code: making time to think critically so that you can become a strategic leader rather than a people, process and operational manager.

Of course, the new leader will have the necessary day-to-day, same-old, same-old stuff in their lives too. There will be some operational To Dos. However, the majority of their time should be taken up with thinking strategically. And the only way they can get to a strategy which results in the participation and operational and tactical actions of everyone else, from sales to marketing, from finance to IT, from manufacturing to distribution, is to learn how to think critically. Critical thinking is the foundation for strategic thinking; it literally supports the development, review, revision and clarification of strategy. As a new leader suddenly everyone expects you to have a big picture, clearly defined set of ideas about the future focus of the organisation. But if you've never had to do much disciplined, critical thinking before, it's a tall order.

Here are the problems:

- You're too stuck in the operation: You are so used to managing the operation that you tend to be too involved in the day-to-day running of your function, department, project, company etc.

- You're too responsive to other people's timings and deadlines: Your managers and team members love you for it, because your high-level, knowledge and experienced involvement helps them to do their jobs. If they get stuck, they simply come and ask you and you, very obligingly rush to their aid. You are so used to having a series of deadlines and tasks with a beginning, a middle and an end, that you find this sitting and thinking business impossible to discipline yourself to do. You discover you'd rather be helping your staff or doing your emails than quietly working on the future of an idea or service or product or plan. That's understandable. Working in the business feels like you are achieving something every day! Working on the business can feel a bit like free-falling; you're not sure when or where you'll land.

- You don't manage your time effectively enough: Critical thinking time has the word 'time' attached to it because you have to take time out of your daily routine, and go somewhere and think. You'll need to make time for critical thinking, often at a period in your professional life when you are going to more meetings than ever and everyone wants a piece of you. And since everyone knows that you don't even manage to get through your emails, how will you find the time to do this critical thinking stuff?

- You don't know how to do it: Critical thinking for many new leaders is something completely new. When you first try to do it, it feels like you are wasting your time, and possibly worse still that you might be wasting precious company time. Surely, you are not paid to sit around and think? Here's the really bad news about using critical thinking to develop business strategy. Strategy is no longer something that is set once, agreed by everyone in the company and then carried out faithfully without deviation, for the next twelve months or few years. Given that the strategy an organisation adopts is simply there to gain sustainable growth, in short to survive and make money, it is unfortunate that this has now become so difficult to do.

Strategy has changed; perhaps forever. It's not just the fault of the recession that has made everyone more demanding and slower to buy and sell. There are other forces at work here; the digital revolution means everyone is connected and everyone can get information. The globally connected, 'flatter' world means that ideas travel and are picked up quickly and there are fewer barriers to entry and globalisation. In a world where competitive advantage can be eroded so quickly, organisations can no longer rely on one, single strategy to develop stable, upwardly mobile growth. Strategy is no longer a one-off, one-time, annual event. At best, it's a roller-coaster ride that is changeable and reactive and it's likely to be built around the all-important customer. To that end, many initiatives and projects may be quite short-lived, perhaps lasting for a year or a season. But they still need a strategy.

That's why critical thinking time is so crucial. If strategies today have to respond to fluid, ever-changing product, service, market and customer conditions, then being able to think regularly, frequently, clearly and analytically about the information you have to trawl through, and being able to turn that into strategic conclusions that provide yet another future direction for the business to take, is absolutely vital.

So here's the good news. You can learn how to think critically. When you do, you will be able to create and re-create strategy, and to justify or defend your thoughts, decisions and action plans when challenged by others. All you need is a process.

The process for critical thinking

Step 1: Identify when your best time of day for thinking about things is. You probably know your body clock well so you'll know at which point you flag physically or get mentally tired, both times to avoid for critical thinking. It's about your unique circadian rhythm, body clock. When I work with new leaders, they all have different time slots individually suited to their own style and preferences. Identify the time that is best for you. That is going to be the time you set aside for your critical thinking.

Step 2: Critical thinking leads to strategic thinking, so accept that this is a beneficial thing to do. Set aside up to two hours every week or every fortnight to undertake some critical thinking. Put this time in you diary and call it 'Strategy Meeting' or 'Strategic Thinking' or 'CTT'. Make it look like something significant, valuable and important so that others who check your diary don't immediately think they can replace that meeting with something they think is more important. Even though you are aiming for two hours every week, you may find that real life gets in the way. If you only manage two hours of critical thinking every three weeks, that is already better than nothing at all.

Step 3: Make critical thinking a habit. Critical thinking can take some time to make into a regular habit. It's a bit like going to the gym. How many people do you know who get a gym membership after a fun-filled Christmas and then they only ever go once? It's the same with critical thinking. You need to think about doing it regularly. When you fall off the wagon, like eating cake on a dieting or fasting day, and discover that a month has gone by without any critical thinking, don't worry and don't give up. Just get back on track as soon as you can.

When should you start your critical thinking sessions? As soon as possible. If you want to hit the ground running quickly then do this in your first week.

I coached a new leader who in her first four days of joining was dragged around from department to department as part of her induction. She simply got up an hour earlier every morning and did her critical thinking time at 6am for thirty minutes a day. As a new leader in a new organisation, her early critical thinking was around her impressions of the organisation and what she thought might be useful information for a SWOT analysis. She made notes every morning about her thoughts and ideas, based on the meetings from the day before. Not only did she undertake the critical thinking, she created a report in her first four days for her new line manager, who was so impressed that 80% of her report was put into effect within her first month. She was promoted within six months and now heads up a business development unit for a group of companies.

Step 4: Find a quiet place to do this critical thinking that is away from your office or working area so that other people can't interrupt you. Some people hide in another part of the building. Others actually leave the workplace and find a café or coffee-house. Some do their critical thinking at home. Wherever you decide to go, find a space that prevents interruption and distraction. Do not stay in your usual work-place. For a start, your brain will be wired to undertake your To Do list or your emails. For another thing, other people will come and ask for your attention and input.

Step 5: When you start your first few sessions of critical thinking, you will find that you are not sure what to do. Don't worry about that. Take some industry reports or thought-leadership papers with you, for this meeting with yourself. Or simply write down your impressions and reactions from your first few meetings and induction/onboarding sessions. Anything that comes up for you has the potential to be really interesting for your peers, direct reports and line managers. That's because your brain is in the 'honeymoon' period, where you are not yet dipped in the new culture and you have some free-thinking around what you are seeing and hearing. Even if your early sessions are simply catching up on Harvard Business Review articles or competitor analysis, you'll find some golden nuggets hidden in the information. And just like the gym, once you get used to doing it regularly, you'll find that your critical thinking muscles get stronger and more focused. In the same way that a piano player has a muscular memory, you will find that your brain soon gets used to using this two-hour slot as an opportunity to think only about future-focused activities which will help create the strategy you need for your organisation's continued survival and growth. Just keep on doing it.

When Rick first started critical thinking, the only time he would allow himself to do it was on a plane journey. A few unbroken hours in a flying tube worked well for him and since he travelled frequently, he soon got into the habit of working on strategy during his flight-time. He even realised during one long, air-borne journey, that a proposal made by one of his team managers, which he had previously consigned to the done-it-before-and-it-didn't-work-therefore-ignore-it pile, might actually work now. The second he stepped off the plane, he messaged a colleague to give him the revised strategy for pulling slow-to-move clients over the line. All the result of some CTT.

Step 6: Critical thinking becomes strategic thinking. Over time, your critical thinking helps you develop strategies. In effect, the lines between critical thinking and strategy-setting become blurred, since being able to do one usually leads to the other. But don't simply think that you are always using these meetings with yourself for setting strategy. What you are doing is taking a step back and connecting with the key questions at the core of your business; those questions that might help it to survive, grow and prosper.

So how do you know if your critical thinking is working? At the end of every session of critical thinking, imagine that you were going to have to present your thoughts to the board or to an exec team or to someone who is of a higher grade or rank than you. Imagine them sitting there, looking at you expectantly and saying, 'Well, what do you think?' Then imagine giving them your ideas and answers. You might talk about what you had read that you found interesting and how that relates back to your team, organisation, product or plan. You might talk about what you see as a problem for the company in future and how you have been thinking about potential next steps. When you imagine having to report back, this can help you to position your critical thinking and give it some direction and vision.

In encouraging my clients to undertake critical thinking, they have come up with new, revised or innovative strategies for everything from team re-structuring to supply chain planning, and from response to changing industry trends, to the creation of new business models. Critical thinking time can be used for any strategic planning that's necessary.

What's vital about critical thinking? That you actually start doing it. Such thinking leads to 'transient advantage'. This is a phrase coined by Rita Gunther McGrath who wrote an article about 'transient advantage' in the *Harvard Business Review* of June 2013[9]. According to McGrath, 'It's now rare for a company to maintain a truly lasting advantage. Competitors and customers have become too unpredictable and industries too amorphous'. McGrath argues that competitive advantage can now occur and evaporate in less than a year, and that the best that can be achieved in a successful organisation is to regularly re-think key strategies so that responses can be more fluid, flexible and customer-centric. What this means is that every leader needs to know how to set, re-position and re-set strategies in order to maintain any sort of competitive advantage. And that's where critical thinking comes in.

Takeaways

1. Critical thinking is the third activity of the code. It's vital that such thinking time should be undertaken regularly by every leader. It's about working on the business rather than in the business.

2. Most people think operationally rather than strategically. Or, they struggle with critical thinking because they are too responsive to other people's needs or deadlines, they don't know how to manage their time effectively, or they simply don't know how to do it.

---

[99] http://bit.ly/1GOqVlJ

3. In order to undertake effective critical thinking time follow the six-step process in this chapter which turns regular, big picture thinking into strategic thinking to help you plan for the future survival and growth of your business.

Chapter 9

Waste management

Any corporate trainer will tell you that the most unpopular, slowest-selling training course is always 'time management'. No one finds it interesting to learn about time management. Daft really. Everyone needs time management training. No one has enough time.

It wasn't always that way. I'm old enough to remember when the fastest means of business communication outside of the telephone, was telex. People under forty don't even know what that is. It's like a cross between a telegram and a fax. It came before the fax. It came before desktop computers, laptops, email and texts. It came before iPhones and tablets. Apart from telex, in the late 1970s, or the 'old days', as my step-children call it, people met each other, or telephoned. Or they wrote a letter, which was posted to the client or supplier or intended recipient. The letter receiver then thought about the contents of the letter, typed or penned a reply, and sent it back. It all took days, longer if you were communicating internationally.

In the 'old days', I used to finish my work around 5pm. I could then read trade magazines, newspapers, reports, letters, books, or any other information before leaving work at 5.30pm. This meant that I could keep up to date with the world, the business news and my background research and analysis for my job. I couldn't really take my office home with me. At the end of the working day or the working week, taking work home meant lugging heavy, overflowing, paper-based files with you; not an easy thing to do unless you had Hulk strength and Arnold Schwarzenegger arms.

Recently, I was delivering a programme on business development skills and a consultant aged around 25 came up to me to ask me how people got any work done before email was invented! The truth of the matter is that, generally, people worked very hard during office hours and were given little time off during the working day to do much else. Of course some work took place outside the office and the 9-to-5 time-frame. However, it wasn't until emails and IM-ing became ubiquitous and we entered the world of constant, never-ending communication that we all had the means to work like Martini (anytime, anyplace, anywhere). I now have clients who call and email me over the weekend. I cannot remember the last time I didn't check my emails or mobile messages whilst on holiday, it's got to be more than ten years ago.

Technology is fantastic. I love my iPhone (internet) and my Blackberry ('phone and email). I love my iPad (play) and my netbook (work). But technology makes us work all the time. In fact, technology makes us work harder than ever. And it is precisely because of this marvellous, technologically-savvy world, that time management is so vital. Particularly for leaders.

I regularly coach senior executives who say things like: 'I am in back-to-back meetings from 8am to 8pm and I usually do my work at home between 10pm and midnight' OR: 'I've had fifteen minutes to myself today and didn't even manage to get anything for lunch'.

So, the fourth activity of the code is all about time management. Even if you think this is the most boring chapter of the book, it's important. Boring and important.

Just to be clear, leaders need to manage their time for three reasons:

1. Everybody thinks that leaders will lead, which means that every other manager will do the doing, so that must mean they have more time for meetings, discussions, tele-conferences and video-conferences etc. Right? Wrong! Everyone knows that leaders have to be more self-sufficient than their predecessors of the 70s, 80s and even 90s, which means that they often do a great deal of their own admin and management as well as everything else.

2. Technology means that there is a constant flow of information which if poorly managed could trip you up, slow you down or overwhelm your working day.

3. Technology means that everyone thinks they can get a response now; right now, without waiting, so everyone will want a piece of you as a new leader.

So here are four tips for improved time management.

Tip 1: Get an Assistant

The first tip for managing your time as a leader is to get an assistant. If you can get an Admin, PA or Executive Assistant who is assigned to you individually go out and celebrate! This person can really help you get organised. And don't just get anyone. Get the best assistant your organisation can afford.

Outside of your personal relationships (with a husband, wife or partner, your best friend and the family members you actually like), this is the most important relationship in your life. A good PA/admin can make your working life run smoothly.

So let's assume you have this wonderful person all to yourself; this is what you do with them.

Email

Make sure he/she is an expert in email, from writing, replying, sending and receiving emails to following an email thread, and also undertaking email filing and archiving.

Encourage them to get on friendly terms with your IT function so that when things go wrong the tech-guys will do everything they can to help. Emails and IT functioning are vital; don't let them disappear into the ether or stop flowing.

Give your assistant as much freedom as you possibly can to open and read all your emails. Use a different email address for really sensitive and confidential activities such as IPO, acquisition, merger or company sale.

Agree with your assistant on some emails that they can deal with and answer on your behalf.

Give them clear lines of demarcation and authority so they know when to come to you for an answer or a decision.

Logistics

Never make your own travel and subsistence arrangements again. If you do, you'll be the most overpaid assistant in your organisation. Give your assistant a few rules, for example your travel and accommodation preferences, time-limits and cost-limits and then let them get on with it. If you can, give them a company credit card to arrange everything such as an American Express card. Amex is good because the Amex Concierge service can do a lot of the work for the assistant, effectively freeing them up to do other things. Amex also offers points which you can give to your assistant as a bonus for their hard work and dedication to making your life easier. Get them to organise everything; taxi, train, hotel, conference, flights, meals, snacks etc.

Meetings

Don't make your own meeting arrangements either. If your boss contacts you directly to talk about a meeting, they should not do that, but if they do, act dumb and pass the challenge to your assistant so that they can sort it out with the admin of your boss. Be clever about your time. Get your assistant to include Critical Thinking Time into your diary, which is blocked out with the same importance and immovability (unless there is an emergency), of any other senior meeting.

Get your assistant to prepare any documents you will need for when you arrive at your meeting. Such preparation might include reports, files, emails, data or even research. A good assistant can create an information pack which will help you to be prepared. And if you agree a look and feel for this information pack, it will be easy for the assistant to use the template and fill in the blanks. Then all you have to do is read, understand and regurgitate at will.

Presentations

All leaders do a lot of their own typing and printing, however, make sure that all time-consuming documents and materials can be developed, completed, collated and distributed by your assistant. You might have to create the content for a presentation but the assistant can give it the right look and feel, and can add the video or audio. In addition, the assistant can help you practice and rehearse, checking timings and accuracy. Whether it's a keynote, PowerPoint, a webinar or a TV or radio interview, the assistant can do a lot of the leg-work for you.

Of course, these are not the only duties and activities of an assistant; others include taking and making calls, acting as a gatekeeper, secretary, mediator with other teams and departments, welcoming and looking after visitors and anticipating drink and meal-breaks, through to carrying out research or maintaining office systems with filing and storage.

However, these four key areas of activity that an assistant can undertake will provide the foundations of solid support that make a real difference to your own time management as a leader.

FAQs

Question: Should you let your assistant deal with your personal life as well as your business life?

Answer: It's up to you. It's a deal you make between you and your assistant. If he/she agrees to pick up your lunch or drop off your dry-cleaning, make sure you are grateful and demonstrate that. Don't expect anything. Personal stuff is not going to be in their contract. If they do support you personally, perhaps you will need to do more personally to say thank you, such as a bunch of flowers if they stay late or a card and gift on their birthday or the anniversary of them being assigned to you. Come to think of it, you should probably be doing this anyway. Keep the assistant on side and they will repay ten-fold your respect, trust and grateful thanks.

Question: Should your assistant get a bonus if their KPIs cannot be measured in the same way as they are in the rest of the organisation?

Answer: You betcha. Agree with HR some kind of KPIs or Balanced Scorecard and make sure that your assistant *does* get a bonus. They will often be far less free to run their own time than any other employee since they have to follow your pace and demands. They will regularly work late, and hold close to them some truly tough and sensitive information. They deserve your thanks and your attention. They earn that bonus.

Question: What do you do if you have to share an assistant with another leader?

Answer: This is a common challenge. The best response to this is to negotiate what you need with your fellow leader and then to agree what you need with the assistant. Of course, if you treat the assistant well, you'll find they end up helping you a lot more than the other leaders; it's human nature.

Question: What do you do if your organisation cannot afford or does not do PA/exec assistant/admin job roles?

Answer: That is also quite a common challenge, although, in my view it is a short-sighted view of the business world. If this is the case, you will need to delegate some of your work-load to others. This is where Tip 2 comes in.

Tip 2: Delegate projects

This tip can be used whether or not you have an assistant. If you can't get access to a PA or admin role it's going to be vital to delegate stuff in order to support your time management and enable you to do your job properly.

Turn as much of your administration and bureaucracy into projects which others can either do for you, or help you to do. Those projects should be given careful prioritisation based on key drivers such as how much X project would save the company money or project Y could make the company money or improve customer retention etc. Once prioritised, such projects could be shared out like a plate of cakes between your colleagues, especially if you are the most senior person on the board or on your team.

You may find that your own specialisms, knowledge and skills make you an excellent project manager for project Z. If that is the case then you could swap projects with your colleagues with both parties concentrating on what they do well. It will take some negotiation, and quite a bit of organising. Not every leader is good at everything. So if you are the best writer in the executive team, and can write quickly and effectively, you could swap a report-writing project for data research that another executive might find easier and more enjoyable than you do. You don't know what other people are into until you work with them for some time or discuss the project potential with them.

I regularly work with boards where one board director will be the main 'writer' for the team, and another is the main 'researcher', whilst another is the 'money'.

If you don't have a PA, you can't delegate the management of your diary, so you'll have to do your own filing and meeting arrangements; although you can use a travel agency or an organisation like American Express to organise your travel. You can get some of your email dealt with if you delegate it to an up-and-coming fast-tracker. This person will have his/her own 'day-job' and will also be tipped for stardom as a future leader in your organisation. As part of their development, encourage them to shadow you and have access to your email, so that they can get used to reading, filing, archiving and responding to certain emails on your behalf. This could be around a key project that they gain sight of.

They would need to be allowed to attend meetings about this project and in return they would be expected to handle the secretarial side of the project. They would also need to read key reports and research, which can also save you time. If they read the relevant report and research and then give you a synopsis, this will be very helpful for you and provide a further development opportunity for them. It is a positive and collaborative way for the fast-tracker to get a sense of what the leadership role would be like, whilst also helping to reduce your potentially overwhelming administration. It's obvious; the more of the project you can delegate, the more this person learns and the less work you have to do on it.

Of course, you need to know how to delegate and what to delegate. The keys to successful delegation include the following:

- You need to know that this fast-tracker is capable of undertaking the work you have planned for him or her.
- You are clear what needs to be delegated and you can explain that to your fast-tracker.

- You give defined authority and demarcation lines on responsibility so that the fast-tracker knows what they can and cannot do and also knows that they can come and see you or call you if they get stuck.

- You agree with the fast-tracker that if they do get stuck, they will come to you with ideas of how to overcome the problems, rather than just dumping the 'monkey' back on to your shoulders.

- You have clearly defined and agreed review points, milestones and deadlines that cannot be changed without re-negotiation between you.

FAQs

Question: Isn't this just exploitation in disguise?

Answer: If you delegate rubbish to the fast-tracker, then yes, it is exploitation. If you genuinely delegate an interesting project or task, then it's a fantastic learning experience. Remember, this whole process ensures that this high potential person gets closer to you, which is exactly what he/she wants.

Question: How can the fast-tracker do their main job properly and also find the time to complete the project/key task for you?

Answer: Make sure they can. Perhaps they could delegate a part of their current job role so that they really do have enough time and head-space to deal with supporting you. There is nothing wrong with a little overtime, but it must not burn the person out. If you are not sure, have a three-way discussion with your relevant, in-house HR business partner and the fast-tracker and agree a way forward that all parties feel is fair and achievable.

Question: What if you want to do all your own work and don't feel the need to delegate; and you decide not to delegate?

Answer: Then, put simply, you're a berk!

When Rick was first appointed to a board role he told me that he got a light-bulb moment after a few days in the role. He said: 'I realised that I'm supposed to be doing the leading, including the critical thinking. And that other people should be doing the doing. If I keep doing everything, not only am I stopping other people from stepping up and improving their game, but I'm a highly paid ops manager rather than a leader'.

Phil Cox, Head of EMEA and India and President of the UK branch of Silicon Valley Bank, told me about the importance of delegation and of walking, talking and acting like a leader. 'Too many leaders keep doing what they're good at,' he said. 'Before my leadership roles in SVB, I worked in one of the top four UK banks and I was the best revenue generator in my business unit. But when I became the BU leader, I carried on being the best revenue generator. It felt natural, and the sales continued to soar, even as I bedded into my leadership role. I worked like an idiot and success continued. But then I got promoted and left the division and the whole division collapsed. What's my lesson? When you become a leader, you have to let go of the fact that you are the best at making the money, managing the project, or dealing with clients; and you have to let other people do the doing.'

Too often, a fast-tracker will take everything that is thrown at them. They never say 'no' to anything and they work and work and work. As soon as they gain a leadership post they find it very difficult to let things go, and they bear the brunt of not delegating to others. Their leadership role is no less time-consuming than their operational role, but they find that their lack of earlier delegation has provided no clear successor to take on their previous role, and no one who can perform in their role as well as they did. You may want to keep the glory of being the best revenue generator on the block, rather than leveraging the help of others or using the scalability of others. But the result is that you'll get stuck in the weeds and you'll be burned out in no time.

Question: Are there any down-sides to delegating?

Answer: Of course. If leaders don't delegate effectively, or the person to whom the work is being delegated cannot perform, then things will fall down or under-perform. As a leader, you will also find that after you delegate you suddenly don't know everything that is going on. You'll start missing some of the elements of the jigsaw puzzle that is your working world. That's a tough one. Most fast-trackers, high potentials and new leaders always want to know everything that is going on with every aspect of their team or function or customer portfolio; but that becomes more challenging the higher up the tree they climb. They have to realise there will be blind spots in the portfolio or the project or the situation. New leaders need to learn how to trust their team and to delegate to them appropriately.

Tip 3: Set time management ground-rules for yourself and others

I know this tip is going to sound like I want you to be a tin-pot general; I don't. It's just that rules of engagement and process do make the world go round. Why else would people spend millions of pounds every year on an IT system, if they didn't think it had value?

Ground rules include things like:

- Setting deadlines for everyone to get information to you or complete reports or allocated tasks.

- Always having an executive summary for every report and piece of written feedback so that you can skim-read it if you are short of time.

- Avoid putting too many items on the agenda of any one-to-one or meeting.

- Making sure you add additional time to your working schedule. Various research on time management indicates that around 30% free, unallocated time should be added to any activity or meeting since there is always some kind of emergency, or crisis or Murphy's law that gets in the way.

- Avoiding 'any other business' as it elongates meetings and one-to-ones. If it's an item for discussion, give it a time slot, preferably at the next meeting.

- Discouraging a 'drive-by' mentality. It's all very well for leaders to say 'I have an open door policy' but this can often be flouted. If people want to drop in, give them between five and ten minutes and then stand up and tell them you have somewhere else to be. If a chat is longer than ten minutes, an appointment should be made so that you can manage your time. If you saw all your direct reports for more than ten minutes every day, you could lose hours.

- Checking email as little as possible and certainly not every time one pops into your inbox. Turn off the email alerts and resist temptation. Ask your PA or admin to check and even deal with at least some of your emails and practice self-control by limiting yourself to three 'fixes' during the working day. Of course, what you do after work, in the comfort of your own home, is up to you.

The value of good time management is really in making sure that you avoid wasting the precious commodity of your own time at work. Until someone finds a way to give us all more than 24 hours a day, it's all you've got. Use it or lose it.

Takeaways

1. The fourth activity in the code for new leader is all about time management. Time management is boring yet important. If you can get an admin, assistant or EA, then delegate email, logistics, meeting preparation, presentations and anything which you can delegate. Don't be an overpaid secretary.

2. If you can't get any admin support, swap projects and tasks with peer colleagues, with each one of you doing what you do best. Where possible, delegate other projects and tasks to fast-trackers, using such delegation to help these people to develop their skills and knowledge.

3. Establish time management ground-rules and procedures for others to follow, such as agreeing deadlines for tasks and meetings and adding extra planning time for task completion, etc.

Chapter 10

Is it me? Yes it is!

I met with Rick at 1pm, and although his PA had agreed that sandwiches would be made available to me since we were working for three hours across the lunch period, nothing was there apart from water. Rick rushed in and when I asked, innocently enough, whether he had eaten lunch he replied: 'Yes. I've had a few sandwiches so we can start straight away'. We began our session; soon Rick was sharing some less-than-complimentary feedback from two of his team leaders about how single-minded he is and how he can leave people behind. I let him talk and then he asked: 'Is it me or are these guys simply not good enough?' I replied without any hesitation or irony. 'Yes. It is. It is you.' He was shocked. But he shouldn't be.

Sooner or later, all new leaders have to learn that they are always part of the problem when leading others. That's because every leader is human and we humans are not ideal specimens. We are flawed, emotional beings, who have used whatever we have to be successful. This often includes considerable talents, skills, expertise, hard work, sheer bloody-mindedness and an unswerving ability to keep on keeping on. Rick has been successful up to now because of how he thinks and what he does. But, as Marshall Goldsmith explains in his excellent book, *What Got You Here Won't Get You There*, when we become leaders, we can find that the very things that helped us to be a successful individual contributor, or a wonderful, operational manager and have become embedded as part of our winning formula are now about to trip us up.

Rick has always been a power-house. He is a perfect example of a lot of new leaders and their belief in what creates success. 'The one thing that will out-trump everything is just to out-work the bastards. You've got to out-work them, out-think them, and out-passion them. But what a thrill.' This quote is from Roy Spence, chairman and co-founder of ad agency, GSD&M.

It's not wrong to be like this. It's just that now, as a leader rather than a manager, for Rick it's no longer enough to work like crazy, and charge ahead with your agenda and your to do list. It's *not* OK to be getting what you want and have everyone else trailing along behind. It's *not* OK for you to have your sandwiches and *not* think about other people and whether they might be hungry. As a manager with a never-ending set of operational tasks to complete such over-work might be the very thing to achieve a deadline. But as a new leader Rick must win over his people and take them with him, not drag them behind him. Being dragged along by someone or something can make you feel bad, rather like an unwilling dog on a leash being taken out for a walk on a cold, wet and windy night. You'll do it, but you won't like it. On the other hand, with a good leader, being given the opportunity to stretch yourself and run a little harder to keep up can feel exhilarating. The fact that Rick had eaten but not thought about whether I had eaten is an indication of his single-mindedness. If he had checked his Outlook entry for that session, he would have read that sandwiches were proposed for both of us during the lunch-time meeting. Instead, he scoffed the lot before coming to see me and I got offered water.

It's a tiny point, but it's a big point. The more senior a leader you become, the more you need to think about your impact on other people. If you live in the 'I'm-alright- Jack' mode, you'll piss off your direct reports and your teams. At best, they will dislike you and be slow to trust you. At worst, they will work to bring you down.

Being new leaders who need to hit the ground running in days not weeks, the Ricks and Janies of this world need to win over the hearts and minds of their direct reports, the teams of their direct reports, the wider teams, clients, customers, stakeholders, their line manager, their line manager's boss; *everyone*.

Over the whole lack of sandwiches episode, Rick was demonstrating to me a clear need for the fifth activity in the code for new leaders; making sure that you think very carefully about the other people around you and do your best to work out what might be going on for them. So when I said, 'Yes it is. It *is* you,' I meant it. For all I know, the two direct reports he was complaining about do have some development needs, but Rick's attitude during that early conversation was a little too shallow and self-absorbed for me to take his words at face-value. If his guys were coming across as not good enough, why was that? What if it wasn't about them but was actually about him?

Another new leader I worked with at the start of his very first managing director role, was irritated by how slow his directors were. He found them over-cautious, over-reflective and overly resistant. After his first week, I suggested that he meet with his board and ask them for open and honest feedback on how well he was doing and what could be improved. Their responses stopped him dead in his tracks. One quote was: 'Bill, you start running across the field and you get to the other side without ever looking back to see if we are following you. You just assume we'll be there. You assume we know what you are talking about and that we agree with you. Stop. Tell us what's going on and why you want to move so fast. Or better still, slow down and find out why we aren't running after you!' That feedback changed Bill's tendency to race ahead. Now he has a sanity check meeting for every key decision where he discusses and gains modification or agreement with his board, before initiating actions. And the board are with him, 100%.

So when you find yourself becoming frustrated with other people's lack of speed, or response or delivery, ask yourself first, 'Is it me?' It just might be. If you want to win over hearts and minds, you're going to have to work out what is going on for other people. What are their challenges, issues, wants and needs?

The signs that you might be missing the needs of others might not always be clear to you. Going back to the dog-in-the-rain analogy, those who are resistant, passive-aggressive, argumentative, in victim-mode or disengaged are probably people who see you as the problem. But what about those who are visibly working hard, performing well and saying and doing the right thing as they always do? Well, these guys are the most at risk when they don't like a new leader. The really good guys, who are high-performing highly effective team members and operational leaders, are the very people who will jump ship and go and get another job, if they don't like you. They don't argue with you; they don't bring you down. They simply vote with their feet. But when they leave, your organisation feels their loss keenly.

So how do you know if the high-performers are seeing you as being part of the problem in the same way as the noisy, overly-sharing, pissed-off performers? Short answer: you don't. So that is why MBWA, team surgeries and winning over key hearts and minds, one person at a time, are all such vital, initial activities for the new leader. You often don't know who has it in for you or who doesn't really like your particular brand of leadership until it's too late.

That's the bad news. Here's the good news. Even if within twenty-four hours you've cocked up royally and your newly inherited direct reports think you are an idiot, all is not lost. If you continue to think out loud, ask questions, brain dump, and aim to connect, engage and inspire, you'll find that this combination of ingredients will work in your favour. You can present yourself and your messages consistently so that most people will see the good in you, the potential in you and the reason to give you a bit of time to prove yourself. You are not aiming for perfect. You are not aiming for everything being sorted. You are aiming for the people around you to perceive you as part of the solution, rather than seeing you as actually making their already difficult lives even more painful, ambiguous or complex.

From now on, whatever senior role you undertake, make sure that you are part of the solution, rather than part of the problem. And you will find that you never again have to use those words: 'Is it me?'

Takeaways

1. Whenever you find that you are asking yourself the question, 'Is it me?' the chances are that it is. It is you. That is why activity five is an important part of the code. It is far too easy for us to see our own plans, decisions, actions and behaviours as correct, perfect or blameless, and to consider others as 'having the problem'. What's vital for new leaders is put themselves in the shoes of the key people around them to understand their challenges, issues, wants and needs.

2. When people seem resistant, aggressive, disengaged or in victim mode, ask yourself if you have said or done anything - or omitted to say and do something - that could be causing this lack of harmony and productivity. Seek to find out the answers and make yourself personally responsible and accountable for changing people's negative views into positive ones.

3. Make sure you continue to undertake your team surgeries and your MBWA, as well as your actions for winning over hearts and minds, one mind at a time. This will ensure that you also win over the people who are already productive and causing you no concern. Always make time for these high-performers because they will be the first to vote with their feet and get another job, simply because they can.

Chapter 11

Come to a HALT

There's so much we can learn from other people, especially recovering alcoholics and drug addicts. For a start, in rehab, they've had to face their demons and they've discovered some cold, hard truths about their own weaknesses. They've also had some fantastic *aha* moments and times when new hope dawns. We are all our own worst enemy, often deluding ourselves that we are worse or better than we actually are, blaming others for our troubles, and cruelly judging and mocking others whilst refusing to deal with our own shit. Addicts have been there and bought the T-shirt and when they get to the other side of the cravings and the ravings, they have some very useful advice.

My learning from addicts came from the early 2000s when I worked for a couple of years at Pinewood Studios, writing e-learning and developing training storyboards and scripts for corporate training and communications programmes to be delivered via private TV networks. These were produced in Pinewood and then beamed out via satellite to groups like BMW, Land Rover and SITA. This was before Sky got going. At the time, Sky had dozens of closed-network TV channels which they allowed business and industry groups to deploy in the delivery of key corporate messaging. I developed source content for the Pub Channel (how to mix drinks, deliver good customer service, and manage unruly customers) and the Automotive Channel (industry updates, health and safety) as well as courses on induction, product knowledge and selling skills for other clients.

During my second year, I rented a room in a private house in Windsor, a few miles from the Studios. The other two room-mates were young men; one an aspiring actor, naturally, and the other an ex-drug and alcohol addict. Whilst the get-togethers were fun and the occasional falling-off-the-wagon crises were emotional, the biggest lesson I learned was from the addict. I'll call him Martin.

As addicts will tell you, getting off the drug of choice is a slow and painful process, and most of them join a group such as AA (Alcoholics Anonymous), where they enter a 12-step programme. This describes and supports their journey towards recovery. During this journey, the addicts discuss the physical and emotional conditions that can lead to a relapse, in other words getting involved in drink or drugs again. These conditions are summed up as HALT or sometimes HALTSSS. The acronym HALT stands for *hungry*, *angry*, *lonely* and *tired*. And the three S's are *scared*, *sad* and *shamed*. If not taken care of, when an addict experiences these conditions, they are more vulnerable and thus more likely to slip back into addiction.

Whilst I'm not suggesting for one minute that any new leader has an addictive personality, what I am aware of is that all human beings have to manage how they are feeling, physically and mentally. If you find yourself in a position where you are experiencing any one of these conditions, they can reduce your likelihood of clear thinking, effective decision-making and results-driven action. Your time, energy and focus end up being frittered away on feeling empty, pissed off, upset, rejected, frightened, miserable or just plain knackered. That's why activity six of the code is so important. You need to understand yourself first and make sure your most basic yet important needs are dealt with. When taking a plane, we've all heard the announcements telling us that in the event that oxygen masks are necessary, we are to put our own mask on first before attempting to help anyone else put their mask on. Activity six is about your own self-awareness, self-protection and self-support. Put your own mask on first.

I always tell new leaders: 'You are a human being first and a business person second'. You can't get away from the fact that because you are not a robot you are at the mercy of how healthy, happy, confident and comfortable you feel at any one time. Your body and brain can literally hijack any decision or action you take if you don't deal with this list. As a responsible, effective leader, you need to be aware of, and manage, your state.

All feelings, whether physical or psychological, can be very good for you. If they are positive, they are good because they can drive you and your ideas forward. And if they are negative, then that negativity is telling you to pay attention and to make a change. So if you are frightened, it might be because you are in danger and you need to get the hell out! If you are hungry, it could mean that you need to eat. Don't beat yourself up for having negative feelings; they are there to serve you. In the same way that a pilot will never fly a plane in a completely straight line and will actually spend 95% of the flight course-correcting, you'll spend your professional and personal life doing the same. Negativity helps you to review, re-calibrate and re-set. (Source: https://hbr.org/2012/12/our-political-leaders-need-a-f 'Our Political leaders need a fiscal flight plan' by Govindarajan and Srinivas 4thDec2012)

So here are some hints and tips on dealing with the times when you come to a HALT or a HALTSSS.

Hungry

You know that you need to put fuel in the car. You know about eating at least three meals a day with high nutritional value. Yet how often do you skip breakfast, shovel down a sandwich at lunch and then gorge yourself for supper? How often do you graze all day, simply snacking on whatever is immediately to hand? UK workers have the lowest productivity in Europe and I often wonder if that's because we don't eat well as a nation and we often don't have a proper lunch break. Ask any French, Spanish, Italian or Portuguese worker; many stop for a full hour for lunch and have a proper hiatus for relaxation, good food and a mental and physical rest. Whenever I work in Paris, I am always amazed at how office doors are locked and open-plan work areas are deserted between 1pm and 2pm, as workers go out to lunch for sixty minutes, even if it's just a baguette!

Tip 1: At lunch-time, whenever possible, find a nearby eatery or café that you can walk to, avoid the in-house canteen or restaurant. This means you'll get some exercise and some fresh air, always a bonus. It also means that you'll be taking a break because you have made a deal with yourself to leave the building.

Tip 2: Have a large salad with meat, fish or cheese or a sandwich which includes salad - and add soup to that. Soup is fantastic because it is very filling and can keep you going for a long time. If you feel fuller for longer, you are less likely to get that afternoon, 'graveyard shift' feeling which has you reaching for crisps, biscuits or chocolate.

And what about other types of hunger? You may also find that you are hungry for attention, for comfort, for understanding, or for connection. For this type of hunger, you need your 'buddy'. A buddy is a person who agrees to act as an in-house, work-based support for you. As a coach, I already have a work buddy in my coaching supervisor. She is someone I can call up at any time if I feel like venting, ranting or whinging. We have a deal; she can do the same to me. So we buddy-up and hear each other's sob–stories on a bad day or celebrate each other's efforts and achievements on a good day. Talking to my supervisor means that I have a ready-made sounding board and I can get clear about what I'm feeling and why I'm feeling it and what my next steps might be. So she definitely gets a call when I need support, or I'm angry or upset, or elated, or scared or well, just whenever I need a pal. If you are a new leader in an organisation where you know people already, you'll be able to find at least one person who can act as your buddy whilst you act as their buddy too. If you are completely new to the company and rock up on day one not knowing anyone except your boss, who, by the way, is not your buddy, then you might need to have a buddy outside of work, like my coaching supervisor. She knows none of my clients. I know none of her clients. But we know each other and that means we can be support buddies. As a corporate, B2B coach, I am very often employed as a new leader's buddy. It's a good call; newbies need support, guidance, advice, a sounding board and an understanding ear. I'm all that and I'm available!

Angry

Most psychotherapists will say that humans in modern society are not very good with anger. Sometimes we have been taught not to show it, and bottled up anger can be physically and mentally toxic. Or we have not learned how to manage it and it spills out and causes damage to everyone and everything around us. Anger is a complex, multi-layered feeling. For example, some people get angry when they observe injustice and lack of fairness. Some get angry when they don't get their own way or when they resent the actions of other people. Some get angry when they feel out of control. Some get angry when they are bullied or ignored or treated unfairly. Whatever form your own anger takes, it's there. When coaching new leaders I give them the good news; anger is normal and natural and can be given a positive outlet.

Tip 1: When you are angry, get up and get out. Don't stay in the room or with the situation. If you do, you might say or do something that later on you will regret. Instead, find an opportunity to go somewhere else. Invent a reason to leave the room or the area. If you can, have a walk around. In anger management terms, this is known as a 'time-out' and the walking around means you have to breathe more deeply. Deeper breathing ensures your body and brain become more oxygenated, which makes you feel both more energised and more relaxed. Counter-intuitive, but true.

Tip 2: When you have left the area where you felt angry, either write or think out loud, alone or with your buddy, about what is making you feel angry. It's possible that your anger is entirely justified. But even if it isn't, it's good to get clear about why you are angry. Mixed up, confused emotions are useless. Clarity is the starting-point for understanding.

Tip 3: Once you know what is making you angry, become curious and interested. Think of yourself as a detective or as an explorer. Ask yourself: 'What can I learn from this? What action can I take that will change/improve/correct this?' and, 'What can I do differently next time?' This may not sound easy to do, but with time and practice, you can quickly overcome feelings of anger by using them as opportunities to benefit and course-correct. If anything in this section has got you thinking that you have some unresolved issues, then talk to your GP or get some Cognitive Behavioural Therapy.

Lonely

Have you ever felt lonely in a crowded room, full of people you know? Loneliness takes a number of forms. You can be someone who likes to connect and talk about things with other people; you are externally referenced and your loneliness comes from the fact that you need other people on a regular basis. Or you could be someone who finds it hard to reach out and connect even when you are with others. Or you may feel rejected and abandoned by the very people you want to connect with. Your feeling of loneliness might be about feeling isolated. The condition of being lonely is actually very similar to that of being hungry. You need to feed the machine. The way not to feel lonely is to have something or someone with which you can feel connected. This is the time to reach out to friends and buddies, whether at work or outside of work.

Tip 1: The best way to manage loneliness is to guard against it. One way to do this is to seek out your buddy and do a deal with him or her, *before* you feel lonely. Agree with your buddy that you will be there for each other. I have two additional buddies in my working life outside of my coaching supervisor, and both of them know that if they need me I will be there for them. And I will always take their calls and answer their emails. I will always meet with them if they ask me to. Offer this and ask for this and your two-way street will provide you with the sense of community that stops you from feeling lonely. Remember the saying from poet, John Donne: 'No man is an island'? Nor woman, for that matter.

Tip 2: If you can't get to your buddy for a sense of community, make a note about how you are feeling and what set it off. Aim to avoid or manage those circumstances better next time. Connect with your buddy as soon as you can so that you can share with them what happened and get their feedback.

Tip 3: By the way, if you are so 'new in town' that you really don't have a buddy, then hire me (I'm expensive but worth it) or another coach, and get them to be your buddy. It works. I have a lot of clients who call me simply for the purpose of having a buddy to talk to. When you have to make people redundant, or fire a nice-but-useless colleague, or close down a much-loved project, you'll soon see why having a buddy is so useful.

Tired

Whilst writing a self-paced learning piece for a client on 'wilful blindness', I read about the factors that can stop our brains from making good decisions. I discovered that one of the biggest culprits in making crap decisions is tiredness. Research has shown that it is common for a person experiencing fatigue to be more rigid in their thinking, to have greater difficulty responding to changing circumstances and to take longer to process information and come up with logical and rational decisions and actions. Focused attention on one thing, to the exclusion of everything else, often referred to as 'cognitive fixation' or 'cognitive tunnel vision', is the typical performance effect of fatigue.

> **Excerpt** from *Wilful Blindness* by Margaret Heffernan. Chapter 4 describes the BP Texas City Refinery disaster of 2005, which caused the death of fifteen people. In investigating the causes of the explosion, the US chemical safety board included evidence that the team involved had been on duty between thirty-three and thirty-nine days without time off; they were exhausted. When people are very tired, they appear to lose the very thing that they need most; the ability to analyse information fully and to make good judgements. Ernst Abbe was one of the pioneers studying the impact of working hours at the end of the 19th century. He concluded that reducing the working day from nine to eight hours actually increased output. As the day gets longer, productivity declines. No study has ever convincingly argued otherwise. Humans need to avoid becoming over-tired or they simply cannot perform well.

When we are mentally tired, both the intellectual capacity and objectivity we need in order to help good thinking and good judgement appear to get lost.

As well as physical tiredness, we can become tired through feeling overloaded and overwhelmed and these are particular issues in the world of work. As a new leader, you are only going to get busier and overwhelm is a very real danger. I won't insult your intelligence by asking you to take weekends off and have proper holidays. You can decide that for yourself. But how can you make sure you avoid getting over-tired when you need to keep going at work?

Tip 1: Take a lunch break for an hour every day if you can. Of course, that may not be possible. If that is the case, then take between one and three short breaks when you can during the day - even fifteen minutes will make a difference. If you can get up and walk around then the oxygenation effect will help; the deeper you breathe, the more oxygen gets into your system and the more refreshed and energised you feel.

Tip 2: Make sure that you are sleeping well at night. This means avoiding anything stimulating for at least an hour before going to bed. So avoid food, heavy exercise, alcohol, action-packed movies or games and any detailed, mental stimulation for sixty minutes before you decide to sleep.

Tip 3: If a heavy work schedule or business concerns are keeping you awake, have a pen and paper by your bed and list all concerns and 'to dos' before you turn off the light. This has the effect of reducing the stress of the issues going round in your head. Even though you may not have been able to sort out any of the challenges you face, the list will allow you some head-space to relax.

Tip 4: If you are really pressurised, form one key question in your head as you lie down and ask your brain to help you with an answer. Then do your best to go to sleep. Your brain is always working, even at night. If it wasn't, your heart would stop every time you went to sleep. When the brain is asked quietly and calmly to focus on a problem at night, it has the uncanny knack of working on it behind the scenes. Many people who have tried this activity have found that by morning they have an idea of an action they can take to progress the issue.

Scared

We get scared for a reason. It's a defence mechanism put there to protect us. So do not ignore the times when you feel scared. Your unconscious brain is trying to tell you something and at the same time it's trying to protect you. Most new leaders are afraid of any new situation where they think they might look stupid or inadequate. Most of us are afraid of letting people down or making a fool of ourselves. Such fear can range from mild feelings of inadequacy through to imposter syndrome. Impostor syndrome is the feeling that you're a fraud and any day now you'll be exposed and is actually very common in new leaders. After all, you're unproven. Perhaps the board made a mistake in hiring you or promoting you? And here is the bad news, getting better at your job and being promoted won't necessarily fix the problem. You've probably heard the phrase, 'The more I learn, the more I realise the less I know'. The great and wonderful Maya Angelou, who died in 2014, said, 'I have written 11 books, but each time I think, "Uh-oh, they're going to find [me] out now"'. Accept that everyone - and I mean everyone - has moments of inadequacy: It's normal.

Tip 1: You've got the drill now. Take a break from what you are doing, move around and aim to work out clearly what it is that is frightening you.

Tip 2: If it's something that has a clear trigger, then decide what you can do about it. Inadequacy can often be quashed by taking some kind of action.

Tip 3: Talk to your buddy, and be honest. Tell them what you are feeling and be prepared to hear that they can match you, pound for pound, dollar for dollar, on their own level of so-called fraud or fear. They'll be able to see your situation clearly and objectively because they are not emotional about it, and they'll be able to help. And you can do the same for them.

Tip 4: Become the detective or the explorer and ask yourself what you can learn from this situation. One high-level *coachee* I worked with was concerned that she didn't know everything about all the financial instruments, products and services in her organisation.

I gave her two actions to take:

1. To decide what she really did need to learn about her company product range and ignore the rest. We don't have enough time or opportunity to learn everything. You know that you can do anything that you want in life, but you cannot do *everything*, there isn't enough time.

2. To find experts and specialists and be open about her lack of knowledge whilst asking for their help. I explained that even if those experts are at a lower grade they would be delighted to share their expertise with her as a leader and that showing she is up for new learning would not do her street-cred any harm. When people admit that they don't know something and seek help to learn, they often gain huge credibility. They have looked a bit vulnerable and human, and they have shown they are open and transparent. People love those things in leaders. In fact, showing your workforce that you *don't* know everything is very good for building bridges and winning over hearts and minds.

Sad

Sadness is also a complex feeling. We can feel sad about things that we observe but are not really involved in such as news of famine or war or injustice. It happens to others but it touches a nerve. Or we can feel sad about something that affects us. Such sadness can have a number of triggers. We might lose someone or something we love or care for, a sense of loss. We may have a problem that makes us feel down and that we cannot put right, a sense of overwhelm. We could feel pain over something that has happened to us, a sense of hurt. Or we might feel discomfort because something doesn't work out the way we wanted it to, a sense of lack of control. Whatever the causes and triggers, sadness is a natural part of our lives and it can be reduced and alleviated.

Tip 1: Do something that makes you happy. Even in my saddest moments, I have found that dancing makes me happy. When my beloved father died at the young age of 56, I told myself that I would never smile again. A friend dragged me out to a club and I discovered that, 24 hours after his death, I was laughing and throwing myself about on a dance floor. I didn't say I was any good at dancing, I just love it. Of course I still grieved for my father, but I realised that, quite literally, life goes on and the things I enjoy can still cheer me up.

Tip 2: Get into flow. Mihaly Csikszentmihalyi is a Hungarian psychology professor, who is best known for his work on flow. His theory states that people are happiest when they are in a state of flow, a state of concentration on the activity or situation they find themselves in. It is a state in which people are so involved in an activity that nothing else seems to matter. The idea of flow is identical to the feeling of being in the zone or in the groove. The flow state is a perfect state of intrinsic motivation, where the person is fully immersed in what he or she is doing. This is characterised by a feeling of great absorption, engagement, fulfilment, and skill. Csikszentmihalyi describes flow as '...being completely involved in an activity for its own sake. The ego falls away. Time flies. Every action, movement, and thought follows inevitably from the previous one, like playing jazz. Your whole being is involved, and you're using your skills to the utmost'.

Work can be a flow activity. So when you feel sad, undertake the activities which provide you with the most flow. That could be number-crunching, report-writing, emails or manuals. Or it could be telephone calls, meetings and discussions. Or it could be creative, innovative or strategic thinking. Whatever it is for you, do it. It stops sadness in its tracks.

Shamed

For the word *shamed*, you can also read *ashamed* or *shame*. Shame is an emotion, like fear or grief. And like other negative emotions it can be painful. Some say it's the most painful of all the emotions, given that research has shown that humans can register shame like a strong physical ache or a stabbing pain.

Shame is also one of the emotions where it is very clear what is going on. When people are ashamed, their bodies show the shame; they visibly sag, becoming smaller and more stooped. Their heads are down and they make no eye contact. Like other negative emotions, shame can be useful because it has a particular role to play in society.

Shame seems to work well in group situations. Thousands of years ago, all humans lived together in communities and had to live in some kind of harmony; being thrown out of the group for bad behaviour might mean the end, literally. So, in today's working environment, shame may occur when others are watching us, and as a new leader you already know that everyone is watching.

Since feeling ashamed feels so bad, most of us will avoid it if we can. We might blame others for how we feel. Or we might try to say and do things that mean we are perfect, faultless, error-free. Of course, we all know that is not possible, but, in a working environment it doesn't stop people trying. People don't like feeling ashamed, so they will work very hard to do, say and be the right thing and that can lead to stress, fatigue and even burn-out.

Now, you might say that as a new leader, during your first few days, you don't have the opportunity, let alone the time, to feel ashamed about something. But bear in mind that all negative emotions have been building up in us since birth and that they are there to protect us and inform us about what to look out for, to avoid or react to. So long before someone judges you in your new leadership role, you are busy silently judging yourself.

William S Gilbert, the lyricist partner of the famous Gilbert and Sullivan duo, wrote, 'You have no idea what a poor opinion I have of myself and how little I deserve it.' That is so true of shame. When we feel ashamed, we really beat ourselves up. Shame can occur when we feel that we look or sound wrong, or aren't part of the team or group or community. We feel shame when we think we look stupid, awkward or fail. Usually, we feel shame and embarrassment because we are worried about what others may think of us. So how can we learn to deal with it?

Tip 1: The next time you feel ashamed ask yourself what is really going on. Are you ashamed because you are judging yourself negatively in the eyes of others who are more articulate, more innovative and more successful than you are? That says something about your own lack of self-confidence or self-esteem. Or are you ashamed because you are being judged by others as a lesser mortal? That surely says something about them; their need to dominate or feel good about themselves by putting others down. Either way, check out what is bringing up your sense of shame, and if you can name it, write it down. When you are clear about your own thinking then seek out your buddy and tell them. You'll be surprised at how much they understand what you are feeling and also at how little they think you deserve to feel that way.

Tip 2: My father was an alcoholic; he would only show me real affection and talk openly to me when he was drunk. But, when he was drinking, and before he got drunk, there was a brilliant window of opportunity when he would say something wise and helpful. Not long before he died of lung cancer, having basically smoked and drunk himself to death, I came home from university in tears, saying I had been told I was at the bottom of my year in grammar, literature, spoken and written language, well, basically I was crap at everything. He held my hand and said to me; 'Let it go, even this will pass'. And he was right.

Think back to the times when you have felt most distressed or devastated. The pain did pass. It might have taken a long time and it might be not very far from your memory, and it does reduce; it does pass. Often, the shame is gone in hours, not days, because something else happens. As a new leader you'll be busy, so get on with it! Time is short. The next time you feel ashamed, tell yourself that this is a transient feeling; one that can be reduced or obliterated over time. Take action, any positive action will do, and the sense of shame will be lessened. If you feel that you deserve to feel ashamed, ask yourself what lesson you can learn and use that lesson pro-actively. If you don't deserve the negative effects of other people's judgements, go and do something physical, like sport or house-work or filing. Or, go and do something intellectual like report-reading or writing.

Tip 3: Make things funny. Smile, laugh and poke fun at yourself. I am naturally clumsy and as someone who is face-blind I am a walking error, waiting to happen. When you cannot recognise people, you can come across as rude or arrogant, or as stupid and ridiculous. Happens to me so much. I used to think I might die of shame. But now, I laugh and joke. I have even written about the silly things I do and my humour is shared with others. The laughter becomes a group event and it feels fine. I won't lie; I feel shame as keenly as the next human being, but I get out of it quickly by laughing at my all-too-human failings. Addicts use these principles to avoid getting dragged back into addiction. We can use these principles to avoid self-sabotaging or to reduce the impact of those nay-sayers whose own lack of confidence means they have to bring us down if they can. When you feel hungry, angry, lonely, tired, sad, scared or ashamed, think about these hints and tips and use them for work, for play, and for all your relationships. Remember that when you start as the new leader you don't have to be cut to the quick by negative emotions and painful feelings. Instead, you can use what comes up for you, to talk yourself into better frame of mind, or to discuss what's going on for you with your buddy.

The key lesson for this chapter is making sure you have a gold-plated, rock-solid, 'I'm-always-there-for-you', friend. Perhaps your best business tool ever!

Takeaways

1. The sixth activity in the code is about taking care of yourself before trying to deal with or take care of others at work. Leaders can learn from anyone, even addicts, who use the principles of HALTSSS to look out for triggers that might make them relapse. It's the same for leaders; being hungry, angry, lonely, tired, scared, sad or shamed are conditions that stop us from performing well.

2. Deal with each of the conditions by following the hints and tips in this chapter and know that these are all natural and normal.

3. Get a 'buddy', probably your best business tool ever! Your buddy is a colleague, friend or coach, but is *not* your boss, with whom you can share your concerns, trials and tribulations. You support them and they support you; it's a two-way relationship to help you overcome HALTSSS.

Chapter 12

Are you an empty Christmas card?

Christmas cards are going out of fashion. Virtually all of our clients now send us e-cards; it's that or nothing at all. So I really like it when a Christmas card turns up at work. It feels familiar, friendly and thoughtful.

So, picture the scene; after a week on the road, meeting clients for Christmas thank-yous and last-minute troubleshooting before the close of play and the December holidays, I drag my carcass into the office and work through my pile of post. Yippee! There is a Christmas card; that unmistakable red envelope with a little holly motif and a carefully hand-written address. Can't read the post-mark. So I rip open the envelope and take out what looks like a high-quality, brown cardboard card which is blank on the front. OK; intriguing! I open the card and inside is: nothing. No words, no picture, no glitter. Zip, zilch, zero. A client has sent us a Christmas card which has nothing on the outside and nothing on the inside. The envelope promised something festive and heart-warming. But inside was a big, fat, let-down.

This empty card is a useful metaphor for new leaders who need to hit the ground running quickly. When you join the new company or the new team, on the outside you probably look and sound the part. It might be the clothes you are wearing, or the words you are saying. That's the red, yuletide envelope. But, if you open up and there is nothing inside, or at least nothing that anyone can recognise or understand, then you might as well be the empty card I received.

Most people want a new leader to do well, even if their initial response is passive, lukewarm or even negative. Most people actually want somebody to follow; somebody they can look up to, learn from and believe in. They want to be inspired by you in your new leadership role. That inspirational leader can be you. You don't need a personality bypass; you don't need to be the cleverest person in the room. You don't need to be the youngest, oldest, smartest or best-dressed person in the game. You just need to do and say enough to make a small difference quickly.

This book is all about speed; the six activities in the code are straightforward, practical and immediately usable. If you want to work with Talenttio, our specialist coaches can help you follow the code. We can also work with you over a ten-day period to guarantee that you'll hit the ground running in your new leadership role. We can make sure that you will do and say just enough to land as a new leader with promise and potential, and a little bit of glitter. Check out our website www.talenttio.com. But you don't actually have to work with us.

Choose the activities that make sense to you and do something quickly and decisively. As long as it's just enough to make a small, yet effective difference, and it's just enough to get the attention of the key players, you'll hit the ground running in days not weeks.

However, if you are all packaging and no content, all show and no substance, you will find that people soon give up on you. Or, worse still, they will actively look for others to connect with or align with. At that point, you're history.

Like any new event, the arrival of a new leader brings hope, optimism and future-focus. But in today's busy, noisy, cut-throat world, where at any moment my limited attention span will be focused on something else, your 'Christmas card' had better land well on the office mat, or pretty soon you'll be consigned to the waste-bin of life or at best left forgotten on some dusty shelf.

That's why it is so important to do and say just enough so that you will get noticed, get remembered and get liked. Make sure you can bring something to your early days of 'show-and-tell'. Do that and you'll do more than survive in your organisation; you'll succeed.

Bibliography

Marshall Goldsmith, *What Got You Here Won't Get You There*: How successful people become even more successful, Profile Books, 2008

Ram Charan, Stephen Drotter, James Noel, *The Leadership Pipeline*: How to Build the Leadership Powered Company, John Wiley & Sons, 2011

Malcolm Gladwell, Blink: The Power of Thinking Without Thinking, Penguin, 2006

John Leach, Survival Psychology, Palgrave Macmillan, 1994

Ben Sherwood, The Survivors Club: How To Survive Anything, Penguin, 2010

Michael Watkins, First 90 Days, Updated and Expanded: Critical Success Strategies for New Leaders at All Levels, Harvard Business Review Press, 2013

Stephen D. Reicher, S. Alexander Haslam, Michael J. Platow, The New Psychology of Leadership: Identity, Influence and Power, Psychology Press, 2010

Peter Fuda, Leadership Transformed: How Ordinary Managers Become Extraordinary Leaders, Profile Books, 2014

Susan Scott, Fierce Conversations: Achieving success in work and in life, one conversation at a time, Piatkus, 2003

Mihaly Csikszentmihalyi, Flow: The Psychology of Happiness: The Classic Work on How to Achieve Happiness, Rider, 2002

Margaret Heffernan, Wilful Blindness: Why We Ignore the Obvious, Simon & Schuster Ltd, 2012

Rita Gunther McGrath, Transient Advantage, Harvard Business Review, June 2013 edition: https://hbr.org/2013/06/transient-advantage

2015 Edelman TrustBarometer, http://www.edelman.com/2015-edelman-trust-barometer/

CMI report.

Coda

In this fast-moving, ever-changing world, just about everything – including a book - is out of date as soon as it's created.

We all have to run to keep up and we all have to keep on learning, un-learning and re-learning. For this reason, from 2016 Henry Rose Lee is running regular, interactive webinars – to keep you up to date with the latest trends, insights and applications in new leadership. They are available, free of charge, to all consumers of this book.

For a full schedule of these webinars, please email books@talenttio.com with the subject line, *Code Webinars*.